Red Road Home

The Outcast Series
Book Four

SUSAN ILEEN LEPPERT

Paperback ISBN: 978-1-956467-12-3
Hardback ISBN: 978-1-956467-13-0
E-book ISBN: 978-1-956467-14-7

Printed in the United States of America
1 3 5 7 9 10 8 6 4 2

DEDICATED TO:

THE WONDERFUL TEACHERS IN MY LIFE.
GOD BLESS YOU.

WITH SPECIAL THANKS TO:

OUR AWESOME LORD FOR HIS MANY BLESSINGS

AND TO OUR LADY

AUTHOR'S NOTE

TO LIVE WITHOUT POSSIBILITIES,

IS TO NOT LIVE.

CHAPTER 1

Even now, months later, Johnny felt an immense sadness when remembering the day he had ridden back into Standing Elk's camp to discover his mother's lifeless body and those of all the others. He closed his eyes at remembering, taking in a deep breath, knowing that as long as he lived he would never forget that day.

His mother had lain face-up, her eyes staring vacantly, limbs frozen, the gaping wound above her left ankle from a saber or sword giving evidence of how she had died. Around her in the snow, tell-tale tracks of a shod horse—a cavalry horse—as it had pranced and danced so near that its rider could end her life with one downward slash of his weapon.

His heart began to flutter at remembering, and he couldn't help but wonder—as he had so many times since—how badly she had suffered. He was certain death had not come quickly. He laid his hand upon his chest in a vain attempt to slow the fluttering of his heart and struggled to take slow, deep breaths; willing himself to calmness. It was a few minutes before his body responded and his heart resumed its normal rhythm. He laid still—eyes closed—his thoughts turning back, once more, to that fateful day.

A few feet from his mother lay his best friend, Brave Foot. His body sprawled face down, knife still in hand. It was plain to see he had been shot more than once, and Johnny was certain he had been running to Sarah's aid when their attacker killed him. He had bent to touch his mother's face, he remembered, not noticing the cold or dampness as he knelt there; his senses numb...so very numb. He'd felt as frozen as her lifeless body, and had no recollection of how long he had knelt beside her. It was as if he, too, had died; the realization of what had occurred so horribly unbelievable.

Suddenly a sound had drifted upon the air; a sound as soft as the snowflakes that had begun to fall. Faint at first, yet startling, in the still silent world of the dead. He had quickly opened his eyes, staring through the falling snow to the rushing water of the stream beyond, in the direction of the sound. A woman's body lay at the stream's edge, and a tiny flicker of movement beside her caught his attention. A baby has survived, he thought, and his heart gave a lurch as he thought of Laughing Water. He rose unsteadily to his feet and began to move as fast as he could through the drifted snow. The child whimpered again, turning toward him; her large dark eyes wide with fear, her small body shaking violently, tiny teeth chattering from the cold.

"It's all right, baby," Johnny soothed, as he bent beside the woman face-down at the creek's edge, knowing she was long dead and he could do nothing for her. It was not Laughing Water, and he felt weak with relief.

He freed the little one's leg from under the woman's body, lifting her up into his arms, tucking her inside his buffalo robe coat so his body heat would warm her. She was trembling, her tiny hands grasping his shirt as she burrowed against him, seeking comfort and warmth. "It's all right. I've got you, baby," he said, and held her to him as he surveyed their surroundings. Feelings of fear washed over him, mixed with a sickening dread that tore at his heart. He wondered if Laughing Water and her children had met the same fate and were lying close by, brutally slaughtered. The baby made soft gurgling sounds, and he patted her gently through the coat, glad she was too young to realize the full horror of what she'd been through. His arm supporting her as she rested against him, he turned and began to walk back toward the camp, intent on seeing if anyone else had survived. His mother, Brave Foot, the two braves he had seen ride through the camp the day he'd escorted his mother on her return to the village...everywhere he looked death greeted him and anger rose up inside him. He wanted to shout for all the children of Mother Earth to hear: *Why?* Dear God, *why?* These were peaceful people! People gentle of spirit. People who did no man—red or white—any harm. *Why? Why?* But there would be no answer. There *was* no answer that could explain something as unconscionable as this.

He came to the body of his mother's friend, Little Moon, and stepped around her, groaning aloud at sight of the bloodstain in the snow that encircled her head. Young boys—not yet warriors—young girls, women and revered elders lay throughout the camp, their bodies frozen in grotesque effigies as if caught in some macabre dance. Their tepees and belongings scattered here and there as if thrown about by a fierce wind. Nothing was as it should have been. Nothing was as he had last seen it, the day he had ridden away, intent on following the guidance in the visions he had experienced weeks before. "I'll find who did this," he stated, and the tone of his voice startled him as it reverberated in the silent stillness around him. Only the soft murmuring of the little one snuggled safely against him within his buffalo robe coat helped to ease some of the pain he was feeling. He hung his head, shaking it in disbelief, then forced himself to walk on.

As he came to the lifeless body of Wind Runner, wife of Chief Standing Elk—her arms still encircling a young boy she had been trying to protect—he heard the thundering hoof beats of many horses. His head jerked up at the sound, and he quickly drew his gun and turned to face those who approached. There was no place to run, no place to hide, so he stayed where he was, not caring that he was now a target if the enemy had returned.

But it was no enemy who rode into camp. It was the braves who had ridden on an early morning hunt with Chief Standing Elk. Their bounty, some deer and an elk, lay across their mounts as they galloped into camp, pulling up sharply on their reins at the sight that greeted them. Shocked to see their loved ones sprawled here and there upon the ground, they stared in disbelief at the realization of what had occurred in their absence.

Chief Standing Elk's eyes caught Johnny's, then looked to the body of the woman who lay at Johnny's feet—his wife of many years, Wind Runner. No expression could be read upon his weathered face, only his eyes betrayed his sorrow as he dismounted and walked over to Johnny. The sounds of grief and anger could be heard behind him from the others, as they discovered—one after the other—the bodies of their loved ones.

"It is a sad day, Black Hawk," the old chief said, his voice soft as a whisper, faltering.

Johnny holstered his gun, nodding, not trusting himself to speak.

"Red Bird?" the chief asked, watching him.

"Over there," Johnny replied, motioning with a move of his head in the direction his mother's body lay.

"I am sorry," Standing Elk said, looking away.

"One has lived," Johnny said, suddenly remembering the little one snuggled safely within his coat. He shifted, using his free arm to open the heavy buffalo robe coat, so the chief could glimpse the child within. Her dark hair tousled, exhausted from the ordeal she had been through, the little one opened her eyes for only a moment, then closed them as she drifted back to sleep.

"It is Spotted Doe, daughter of Morning Dove," the chief stated, his voice breaking. He shook his head, his eyes growing moist. Then he looked at Johnny, studying him. "You are not hurt?"

"No. I arrived...after," Johnny replied, his words stilted.

4

"The bluecoats kill our women and children and our elders, shooting them down like dogs. It makes my heart feel great sadness," the old chief said. "Many moons ago I had a vision. In this vision I saw many of the People laying dead, as on this day, and great sadness filled our village.

"There followed a great war. Many nations rode together as one. When it was over all the bluecoats lay dead." He paused, looking off to the west. "I have seen this and now know it was a true vision." Behind him the keening sounds of death songs filled the air. Then the old man looked directly into Johnny's eyes—a look he would never forget. "You carry the blood of *both* people, John Black Hawk Gentry. From you a decision must be made. It will not be an easy one, but one only you can make. Whatever you decide, you will always be welcome in the camp of Standing Elk. Take time to think on these things," he said, reaching out a gnarled hand to touch Johnny's shoulder, a look of compassion upon his face as he studied him.

Johnny met his gaze, remembering the kindness and caring the older man had always shown to him and his mother. He recognized the wisdom in the old chief's words, as he had many times before. "I need no time to think. The decision was made for me when the bluecoats struck down my mother and the others," Johnny replied. As of today I am no longer John Gentry. As of today, I ride with the People, known only as Black Hawk!"

CHAPTER 2

It did little to ease Johnny's grief when he finally discovered Laughing Water and her children, safe and sound, later that day. He had searched relentlessly among the dead, his heart hardened by sight of the carnage: elders, their dead eyes staring as if in disbelief, young mothers cradling between stiffened arms their dead babies. He walked among them, feeling with each step a growing anguish. Overwhelming grief, that was what it was, he thought. Once before he had thought he knew what grief was as he journeyed mile after mile, searching for his father after the war. But that hadn't been grief, he now realized, only overwhelming disappointment. This—this *butchery* before him—was a grief beyond *anything* he could imagine. A grief that choked the breath from a man, tearing into his soul, ripping a hole in his heart that would not— *could not*— be healed.

When he came to Howling Wolf's dwelling, he cried out at sight of his father's old friend. Howling Wolf lay on his side, his bow still gripped in one stiff hand. Johnny bent, touching his friend, his vision blurring with unshed tears as he saw that Howling Wolf's head had been almost completely severed by a saber's blow. He turned away, vomiting, as tears began to course their way down his cheeks. Anger, raw and vicious in nature, rose up in him. He stumbled, shuddering violently, blind with rage at the injustice he was seeing.

It was then that he thought of the cave where he and Brave Foot had played when they were young. The cave that he had told Laughing Water about only days before. A small glimmer of hope suddenly filled him. He turned in the direction of the cave, hoping beyond hope that she would be there, hoping beyond hope that she and her children would be alive and uninjured.

The absence of any tracks leading toward the cave caught his attention as he approached it. His heart pounded in his chest like a drum as he entered, drawing his knife from its sheath, not knowing what to expect. There was an eerie silence as he crept stealthily along, his back to the wall, his breath held. He listened, ears straining for the least sound. All was quiet. Then suddenly a scream broke the stillness, and a form hurled itself at him—tomahawk in hand—as it sliced the air near the side of his head. He grabbed the hand that held it, crying out—first in surprise, then in relief—as he saw it was Laughing Water who wielded it. "Laughing Water," he uttered. At the same time she realized it was Johnny. She dropped the tomahawk and rushed into his arms, shaking from fear, her tears wetting the front of his coat. He held her to him, his own body trembling now from the relief he felt in knowing that she was alive—alive and safe within his arms. He held her tightly, never wanting to let her go.

"Did I cut you?" she asked, when she could finally pull herself from his embrace.

"No. You came close," he replied, still unable to believe that she was standing in front of him, unhurt. "Are your children..." he started to ask, but she nodded toward the back of the cave, in answer. He reached out, once again, to touch her: her face, her arms, her shoulder, and sighed, gratitude filling him.

"I heard many screams," she said then, her voice soft, her eyes asking questions he could not bear to answer. "Brave Foot will be looking for me and..." she began, her words ending in mid-air as she saw the fate of her husband in the eyes of the man who stood before her. The man she so loved. She moved back into Johnny's arms, fresh tears trailing a path down her cheeks. "He was a good husband. A good *man*," she said, her voice soft as a whisper.

Yes. And a brave one," Johnny added, knowing *she* would sing Brave Foot's death song, and *he* would build his burial scaffold. And in years to come, he would tell her children of the bravery and many fine deeds of their father and of the friendship they had long shared. At the soft whimper of her littlest one, Laughing Water turned from Johnny to tend the infant. He watched her pick up the child, thinking of the little one he had found that morning, and had wrapped within his buffalo robe coat. He had given the tiny girl to a young woman he'd found wandering among the dead, searching for her own missing child. She had stared at him a moment, then clasped the little girl to her, nodding quickly, then hurried away. Johnny remembered wondering then if she had been too distraught to realize it was not *her* child she held, but another's. But what did it matter? he thought. The woman had spoken softly to the child as she walked away, and the baby had mewled in response, then snuggled against her, each filling the other's need.

Johnny looked at Laughing Water and her children, thoughts rushing back to his *own* childhood and the tender love he had always been shown by his mother. As plain as if he were standing at their home near Hastings, he saw Sarah Gentry shucking peas into a large bowl out by the barn. "Johnny, be careful you don't fall," he heard her call to him as he climbed ever higher in their old apple tree.

"I'll be careful, Ma," he had answered, just as the branch he was balancing on gave a sharp snap—sounding more like the crack of a rifle—and he found himself dangling by one hand to the limb above him. Before he could cry out, his fingers had begun to slide, one-by-one, and down he went—head over heels—landing with a thud on the hard ground. The wind knocked from him, he gasped for air, clutching his chest, a loud whirring sound in his ears. Then he was being lifted into his mother's arms as she clasped him to her. She rocked back and forth, holding him tightly, and he could see her thoughts written plainly upon her face. He struggled to speak, but couldn't, his breath still labored. It was then he realized the depth of her love for him. *That*, and something else...*fear.* It was the look in her eyes...the haunting look of loss his fall had caused her. He knew it for what it was then, that look...it was as if *he* and *he alone* was all that she had, to give her the strength to go on.

He was only seven then, but in that moment he saw clearly the tremendous loss she had felt by his father's leaving to go to war, and the immensity of her love for *him;* their son. "I'm all right," he managed to say, at last, knowing he was in for a whooping for scaring her so badly. But she only knelt there, holding him tightly, tears tracing a path down her cheeks. "I got the air knocked out of me, that's all," he said, when he could speak. "I won't climb that old tree again. I promise," he added, and felt her loosen her grip. She took a deep breath, running a hand through his hair, getting control of herself, then smiled at him and returned to the bowl of peas.

He brushed himself off, filled with an awareness he had not had before. He had never seen his mother like that: afraid. She had always been strong, fearless, able. She could shoot—almost as good as his pa—and stood her ground when troubles were afoot. Yet that day he had seen what his pa's leaving had cost her. It was as if her strength had gone with his pa, he remembered thinking, and now she holds firm to *me.* He smiled at the memory, knowing he had never again climbed that old tree. Not because he didn't want to, but because he never wanted that look of fear to appear on his mother's face again. Abruptly his thoughts changed, jarring him, as he wondered suddenly if she had been filled with an even *greater* fear when the soldier was...No!, he couldn't let himself think about that. He shuddered, looking back toward Laughing Water as she quietly approached.

"We should go see to the others," Laughing Water said, her voice soft.

Johnny looked at her, hearing the hope in her voice. Not able to stop himself, he asked, *"What others?"*

In one deliberately brutal act, their lives had been changed forever. There would be no going back. There was *nothing* to go back to. Life— as they had known it—was over. His mother had been all the family he had. Now she was gone. He would bury her here among the people she had loved and had chosen to share her life with. Then he would go in search of the man who had killed her. He walked from the cave, driven by his desire for revenge, wanting death for the bluecoat responsible. He couldn't let himself think further than that, would just do what he had to. Tormented by the feelings that raged within him, he halted suddenly as he came again to the body of his father's old friend, Howling Wolf. He stood there, filled with an anger unlike *any* he had ever felt before. Then he bent down, placing his hand on Howling Wolf's shoulder, and the tears he had held inside all the long day poured from him.

CHAPTER 3

A tear fell onto John Gentry's cheek as these memories flooded his mind. It wasn't only the memory of his mother that day, months before, or of his friend, Brave Foot. Nor was it the memory of the savagery done to Howling Wolf that tore into him, ripping at his heart. It was because of his *own* actions that day. The memory of it had tormented him ever since. He doubled his fists as he remembered, shame filling him. I was out of my mind with grief, he thought, knowing it was not the first time he'd tried to ease his sense of guilt with that very same excuse. He was not conscious of the fact that he was clenching and unclenching his fists upon the blanket that covered him. He closed his eyes, squeezing them tightly shut against all the memories. But it was no use. Clear as day he saw—as he had so many times since—the scene that thrust itself into his mind, causing a wealth of grief and sadness.

He had knelt there beside Howling Wolf, unable to control the tears that flowed down his cheeks. His shoulders shook and he was aware of nothing around him, only of the unbearable grief and sadness he felt. Even the sounds of the others grieving, wailing, and singing their loved ones' death songs were blunted from his mind by the intensity of his own grief. And then—as if in a moment of awakening—he realized Laughing Water's hand lay upon his shoulder, her voice soft upon his ears, her words meant to comfort . . . "Johnny? Johnny…"

"Leave me alone," he said, as he struggled to get control of his emotions. He'd said it in a way that left no doubt but that he'd meant it, and saw surprise written upon her face. "I'm sorry," he said, taking a deep breath, then reached out to take her hand. But she stepped back and away from him, her posture stiff, back straight.

"I will go see to the others," she said, not looking *at* him, but at the ground, as she turned and quickly walked away. He couldn't help but see the sadness he had caused her, yet stood silent, still too angry and hurt to do anything more. Watching her go, her baby boy in his cradleboard upon her back, her little girl stumbling along at her side, she paid him no heed as she crossed the snow-covered path, stepping across the bodies that lay in her way. He called after her, wondering if she would turn and come back to him, but it was not to be. She was a stronger woman than most. That was one of the reasons he had fallen in love with her. She had reminded him of his mother, who had always been thought of as both strong-minded and strong-willed. It would take a good deal of apologizing to gain her forgiveness, that he knew, but he was not in an apologizing mood. There were enough burdens to tend to, *more than enough* to lay a man low, and that was the truth. I'd better tend to Ma's buryin', he thought, trying to get his thoughts in some workable order. He glanced in the direction Laughing Water had gone, seeing a pair of buzzards land beside a young boy's body. First things first, he thought, and ran to chase them away.

As he dug his mother's grave in a grove warmed by the sun and not far from the stream near where she died, his anger spurred him on. Every shovelful of dirt was propelled by the burgeoning anger that rose up in him, casting out all other feelings. Death would come to the man who had killed her, that was the silent promise that lifted each shovelful of dirt. A painful death, if he found him. And he would. He *would* find him, he vowed, and *inch-by-inch* make him pay for the pain he had inflicted. An eye for an eye, that was what he wanted. No easy death would he get. No easy death, by any means. Johnny had seen the track the soldier's shod horse had left; the small mark like an "x" on the edge of its shoe. He would find that soldier if he had to look for him all the rest of his life. And when he found him, he would kill him, and be pleasured by doing so.

Finishing, at last, he placed one last rock upon the pile of dirt so no critters would get at his mother's body. Then he hunkered down beside the grave, wiping the dirt from his hands, his eyes threatening to once more fill with tears. Where do I go from here, Mother? Do you know the grief I feel in my heart? His thoughts tumbled over and over in his mind, as a weariness spread throughout his body. The anger he had felt now turned to a smattering of fear as he realized he was all alone now. There was no family for him to go to. No family to claim him, welcome him or share his grief. No family to care if he lived or died. Pa would have known what to do, he thought. And it saddened him further, knowing his pa had died long before, and now he was truly alone.

The image of Grandpa Angus suddenly entered his mind; his soft white beard so real that for a moment Johnny felt as though he could reach out and touch it. But he knew he could not. He closed his eyes, hanging his head, waiting for...he knew not what.

"Ye've got t' be a man now, Johnny," he heard Grandpa Angus say, as he had said once before, when Johnny had been just nine or ten. When the war had ended and his Pa had not returned. "'Tis a load only a man can carry, tha' the good Lord's seen fit t' place upon yer shoulders. Ye've got t' be brave, lad, and strong." Johnny kept his eyes tightly closed, hearing the rich Scottish brogue of his grandfather as clearly as if he stood beside him.

"Oh, grandfather," Johnny whispered, "if only you were really here." There was only the wind echoing through the trees for answer.

The wind, and the keening sound of the others who grieved. He stood, moving his legs to work the stiffness out of them, then strode over to a tree to break a branch from it. He broke it in two: a small piece and a slightly longer one. Then tied them with a piece of rawhide from his pocket, forming a cross. Not fancy, he thought, but adequate for the time being. He would have liked her to have a nice headstone, would have liked her to be in the cemetery beside his grandparents. But she had chosen the life she had shared with Standing Elk's People. Had chosen to live with them, and in doing so, had died with them. Much as it hurt him, he knew his mother had made her choice, and there was no changing it now. Hat in hand, he stood beside her grave, shoulders hunched, wanting to whisper the prayer she had taught him when he was small. But the only words that came from him were spoken from the hate that had only just begun to fester within him, "I'll get him, Mother. I give you my word. I'll get him."

CHAPTER 4

Hastings was booming by early winter. The steamboats brought more and more folks to town, as did the railroad. Business men, homesteaders, and other enterprising individuals came, as did wagon after wagon, filled with exhausted families. The strain and weariness showed plainly upon their faces, often obliterating the looks of hope they had once held. The hope of starting anew in this land of promise where they would own their own land and prosper. A land where opportunities abounded. Gathering the supplies they would need and all their belongings—necessities and dearly cherished items from dear ones they had left behind—they had set out, intent on their faith, their fortitude and their will to see them through the journey that lay ahead. Men, weathered from long days in the saddle, their tired bodies seeking a game of chance, a place of rest, a welcoming saloon, and often the companionship of a lady, rode into town. The dust and grime of the trail evident upon their clothing, horse and gear. Guns hung at their sides, rifles next to their saddles. The jingle of spurs and creak of their tack—though one had to listen carefully to hear—giving off an assortment of sounds, discordant in nature as they rode along.

Cal Dunnevey smiled contentedly as he stood inside the Mercantile watching all the activity out in front. Horses, heavily laden, whinnied as they struggled to pull loaded buckboards and Conestoga wagons down the street, snow-filled ruts hampering their progress.

Whips cracked, men shouted, women kept vigil over excited and curious children, their faces showing concern, worry or determination. Or was it resignation? They were a strong lot, these men and women who ventured west. Strong in mind *and* strong in body. Cal could only imagine the strength it took to face all that might lie ahead for them. Why as strong as his wife was, he couldn't imagine Ophelia pulling up stakes and leaving all her loved ones behind, to follow a dream. He smiled, knowing her Aunt Hilda would never hear of such a thing. He could just imagine the tongue-lashing she'd give him if he ever once proposed such a move. Auntie Belle, bless her heart, he thought, would probably be just the opposite. She'd probably start right in to packing. He laughed aloud at this thought. Auntie Belle had more spirit, more spunk, than a *dozen* other gals her age, and he loved her for it. Her soft—almost child-like—laughter when something caught her fancy, as well as her bright and bubbly spirit…what joy she brings to each day, he thought. I've grown to love her nearly as much as my sweet Ophelia. Then he turned away from his reveries as the door flew open and a short, well-dressed man entered. He stood approximately five feet five inches tall, Cal guessed, slim of build. Clean-shaven with pale skin, turned up nose, and thin brown hair combed straight back, he wore a black frockcoat over a white shirt and dark suit. Except for badly scuffed boots, he was quite impressive looking. A black derby hat perched jauntily upon his head, and he carried both an ornately carved cane and dark brown leather valise. The contents appeared to be quite heavy, as he shifted it often, from one hand to the other. When he spoke, he looked directly at Cal, never blinking or taking his eyes from him. His voice was soft, though high pitched, and Cal knew at once his heavily accented drawl lay claim to a southern origin.

"Good Morning, sir," he said, sir sounding more like "saw." "Might you be the proprietor?"

"Good morning to *you*, sir," Cal replied. "Indeed I am." He reached out to shake the man's hand. "Cal Dunnevey at your service," Cal stated, smiling.

"Cornelius T. Attbury, purveyor of hopes, dreams, and often properties." He saw Cal's questioning look, and quickly added, "I'm a lawyer, by trade, sir. Would ya'll be so kind as to tell me where I might acquire lodging and a meager repast? It's been an unexpectedly long and arduous journey, from my home in the glorious state of South Carolina, to your fine town of Hastings."

"Yes, Mr. Attbury, I certainly can," Cal stated, finding it difficult to keep from smiling at the thought that Cornelius T. Attbury looked—in his black derby hat and white shirt front—not unlike a penguin that he had seen in a book, years earlier. "You can get a fine meal, sir, at the boardinghouse just across the street."

"Thank you kindly, Mr. *Dunnevey*, is it? Yes. Yes. Dunnevey. Hmm..." he studied Cal a few moments before stating, "I shall *see you* again, sir. Thank you for your kindness. Good day." With a slight nod of his head he turned and left the store, walking quickly across the street, hurrying to dodge a fast moving buckboard.

"Well, what a strange little man. I wonder what that was all about," Cal said aloud, as he rubbed a hand across his eyes, trying to alleviate the slight blurriness and pain that came whenever he felt the least bit tired. Not one to complain, he was more than a little thankful that at least he could see. What was a little pain and blurriness, he thought, compared to how terrible it had been when he was blind?

The memory of the gunfight that had left him blind, still played in Cal's head. He tried not to dwell on it, or the terror he felt every time he remembered, but once again he could feel his hands grow suddenly clammy and sweat bead upon his brow. Though there no longer was an accompanying stab of pain that flashed across his temple—jarring pain that twisted his gut and rendered him helpless against its ravages—he felt the dreaded, all-encompassing memory of the blackness it left in its wake. He was glad the Santiagos were dead. Glad that Lea was free of the horrible mistreatment they had put her through. But he had not reckoned on the devastating turn of events that would change his life so completely. If only, he thought, and he rubbed one hand across his forehead, taking in a deep breath. Staring out at the street, he saw once more that day so long ago…

The colorful beauty of the sunrise that day, and happy look spreading across a customer's face. The gracious smile of greeting, and the endearing grin of her impish child, as his mother shopped, and then Amos had come, saying it was time to go. Time to face Lea's husband and sons: the Santiagos.

The deafening blast of guns and searing pain, as he felt himself falling back, conscious only of the immense pain that tore through his head...and then...the horrible, horrible blackness. Endless blackness. Terrifying blackness. The smell of gun smoke hung in the air, and he'd heard Moses swear, then call his name, and then there was nothing, nothing but the blackness.

No longer could he see the reds and yellows of sunrise and sunset. No longer could he see the changing blues of sky, or beautiful shimmering rays of sun, or green grass or lovely windswept golden prairie grasses he had so enjoyed. Gone, all of these treasured things in one earth-shattering explosion, robbing him of all the many beautiful things he had taken such pleasure in seeing. Robbing him, too, of so much more: of his confidence and trust. If it hadn't been for the gentle care from Ophelia, he thought, it would have robbed me of my life. He had become a bitter man; a man bereft of joy and happiness, left with a mood as black as the world he found himself thrust into.

Moses had been sheriff then, Amos Culpepper his deputy, as the three of them walked up the street—dust swirling around their feet—to the stand-off with Diego Santiago and his sons. Three against three, though *he* had been a greenhorn compared to Moses and Amos. He slowly shook his head as he remembered. If it hadn't been for Lea. If I hadn't loved her so, he thought, closing his eyes, feeling an intense stirring of his heart. His whole world had centered around Lea. It wasn't her fault...any of it, and yet...

Doc Valentine had explained that, yes, there was hope, that someday, *possibly*, his sight might return. But he winced at his words, not believing them. Life was going on around him, but for *him* life had stopped. He shuddered, remembering the intense grief and anger he had felt when, at last, Doc unwrapped the bandages covering his eyes, and he could not see! He'd held his head within his hands and wept. Lea had rushed to his side, attempting to comfort him, but he shrugged her hands away and turned his face from her, not wanting her to see him cry. Not wanting her to see the man he had now become.

"Cal," she softly whispered, her voice as plaintive as a child's. He knew without seeing, that her bottom lip was trembling. "I'm so sorry," she said, and he felt some of her tears upon his wrist. "I didn't mean for this to..." she started to say, but he pulled back from her.

Wiping his face on the arm of his shirt, moving unsteadily, he got to his feet, embarrassed by his lack of confidence that grew worse every moment, answering, "I'm fine," his tone sharp. "Just take me home," he demanded.

"Doc?" Lea questioned.

"Good idea," Doc replied, a sad smile upon his lips. "Get some rest, Cal. I'll come over and check on you tomorrow, to see if the headaches have stopped. Oh, here, take this, Lea," he said, handing her a cane for Cal to steady himself with. She took it, touching Cal's arm with it. He took it, but not before his hands stroked the air, trying to find it. A grimace upon his face, he yanked it from her when he had finally discovered its whereabouts, then turned quickly, bumping his hip painfully on the table's edge. Angrily he brushed Lea aside, then groped for the doorknob. Finding it, he nearly collided with a passerby, as Lea took his arm to guide him. He said nothing as they made their way across the street, but was acutely aware of the sounds all around them. The hoof beats of passing horses seemed frighteningly close and dreadfully worrisome, causing his heart to pound. Smells of sweat, perfume, body odor, food cooking somewhere, dung, lye soap, sharp odors, sweet odors, all assailed his senses. Worst of all was the endless cacophony of noise—not normally distracting—that also caught his attention: the squeaking of saddles, the clank of a bridle, the stiff creak of leather stirrups, and the voices and laughter that filled the very air around him. He wished he had *not* gone that day. Not even for Lea...

He remembered then, the day he had asked her to take him out to his property. Remembered how she had to help him up into the buggy and back out of it, as if he was an invalid. Once there, *even there*, he could get no comfort. Even there his spirits had not lifted, though he could smell the flowers at his feet and the strong scent of pines to one side. He felt ashamed at his helplessness, and going there had dashed his hopes even more so. He closed his eyes, taking in a deep breath, great sadness filling him at remembering.

She hadn't been *his* Lea. Had *never* been. Would *never* be. He was married now to her sister, Ophelia. Married to the woman he had *grown* to love, as she nursed him back to health after Lea had left. After *he* had driven her away. A sigh escaped him at these memories. He never knew, back then, that a day might come when his sight would be restored. He had never even *dreamed* *such* a day would come. If he had known... if there'd been even the *slightest* promise of such outcome...but no, at that time he *had* no such hope, no hope at all, and he had screamed at her that it was *her* fault. He could still remember the way her small body had trembled in his arms, as she begged him, pleaded with him, told him she loved him and that his blindness didn't matter. And he had thought only of *her*, of what life would mean for her, if she married him—and had to live with his blindness. The cutting words he had hurled at her—meant only to free her from his world of blackness—tore at her as it tore at him now, and he not only *knew*, but *felt* the pain he had caused her. She had turned and ran from him, from his embrace, and from the love he had felt for her...undying love...love that tore at his heart *every time* he thought of her and that day, so long ago. "If only I'd have known my sight would come back," he whispered under his breath, and then reality coursed back. He was married to Ophelia now, dear sweet Ophelia, Lea's sister. No woman could be more caring, more loyal, or self-sacrificing then Ophelia. *His* Ophelia. The wife he had grown to love. He owed her so much, was so grateful for every moment she had been there during his long stay in the hospital, nursing him tenderly back to health. Cal drew in a long, steady breath, no longer lost in the past. He coughed to clear his throat, "It's time I'm getting for home. Ophelia will have supper waiting." He glanced around the Mercantile, then once more out into the street. But it's always been Lea, he thought, from the very first moment I saw her. And sadly, even the love I feel for Ophelia hasn't changed that.

CHAPTER 5

Ophelia Dunnevey rushed down the hallway of the hospital, dirty dishes filling the tray she held in her hands. The last of the patients had now been fed, and she knew she would have to hurry to get washed and have supper on the table before Cal arrived home. Living at the hospital had been no problem when she was unmarried, but as a married woman now, she felt pulled in two directions. It was, after all, her responsibility to see that each patient was cared for to the best of her ability. And yet, she knew she had a responsibility, just as important, to her husband. Cal never complained—she was thankful for that—when she had to rush off to care for a patient, or to comfort a grieving family when a dear one succumbed. He would nod and smile in that sweetly understanding way of his, as she hurried off to tend to whatever needed her attention. Sometimes she expected a word of rebuke from him, but so far he had given none. She was glad. She so enjoyed running the hospital. The Johnathon Clark Hospital. How proud Johnathon would have been, she thought, a smile crossing her face. Sitting the tray on the cupboard, she pushed an errant strand of her hair back, standing still, surveying the small pile of dirty dishes in the otherwise clean kitchen. She could smell the delicious scent of venison stew and biscuits that filled the room, not to mention, the aroma of the doubled crusted apple pie that sat on the window ledge. Auntie Belle had made eight pies that morning, and this was the only one that was left. It would please Cal, being his favorite dessert. She wiped her hands on her apron. "I'll have to hurry if I'm to freshen up before Cal gets home," she said, speaking softly, and she turned and rushed up the narrow stairway to their rooms.

What a lucky woman I am, she thought, as she quickly washed and changed from her soiled skirt and blouse into a clean dress of light blue calico. Aunt Hilda had bought the material for it, and dear Auntie Belle had sat up late into the night, many nights, sewing it for her. She pulled it over her head, noticing for the first time how the fabric felt oddly tight—almost constricting—over the slight fullness of her belly. Why, I'm getting fat, she thought, running a hand over the newly dis-covered fullness. She walked to the long oval mirror at the end of their bedroom near their heavy oak bed, glancing at herself from the front and then from the side. "Well, how can that be?" she questioned aloud, knowing she was often so busy with patients that she neglected to eat her lunch, and often was too tired of late to finish her evening meal. "I don't understand it," she said, and suddenly her mouth opened in surprise as she realized that her monthly had not occurred since... when was it? She sat down upon the bed, silently trying to figure back. She placed her hands on each side of the slight bulge that had always been the flattest of flat stomachs. Had she really been so unaware of her own courses that she was with child—had been for some time—and only just now realized it? Thoughts flooded her mind, both frightening in a way, and then—suddenly—so joyful. "After all this time, and as old as I am," she whispered into the silence of the room. "I'm going to have a baby." Tears began to fill her eyes at the reality of her pending moth-erhood. She had thought of herself as a spinster schoolmarm so long. Even after her marriage to Cal, she had not once taken the time from her heavy schedule of responsibilities as head of the hospital and as his wife, to consider that someday she might have a child. It wasn't that she didn't want one. True, the events of her own childhood—her mother's death and father's excessive drinking—had deterred such thoughts and led to the decisions she had made for her life. The decision to come to Hastings, first of all, and then to apply for the position of teacher. Then, years later, Johnathon's death and his gracious gift to her; the bequeathal of his beautiful home… which now, of course, was a hospital named in his honor.

She rose and walked to the window, looking out at the snow that had begun to cascade down, covering everything in a lovely blanket of pristine white. The baby should be due in early spring, she thought, as she ran a hand gently across her belly. Picking up her brush from the table near the window, she began to brush her hair, a feeling of immense joy filling her. How many nights had she enjoyed the bliss of her marriage bed, never dreaming a man could pleasure his wife so, until she and Cal had wed. A warmth rose up in her at these thoughts. Cal was always so gentle with her. Never had she expected their coupling to be so wonderful. It was a joy beyond any she had imagined every time he took her into his arms and held her, whispering words of love and promise, easing her fears and stirring her to unimaginable heights of surrender. Oh, how I love you, my husband, she thought. I'm so thankful for you...and now...for our baby.

"Ophelia, where are you?" Cal called from downstairs, causing Ophelia to jump. Setting the brush aside, she straightened her dress and hurried from the room to greet him. "My, don't you look pretty, wife," he said, as she rushed down the steps, smiling at him. He couldn't help noticing something different about her, though he couldn't quite place it. She seemed to have a glow about her, an inner radiance. He returned her smile, wrapping his arms around her and holding her close. As their lips touched, a warmth grew within him, stirring the passion they had always experienced between them. If we had our own house, he thought, I'd take her straight to bed, forgoing our evening meal until *much* later.

Ophelia was the one to pull away, ending the growing warmth that both felt. "I'm sorry, Cal. I got preoccupied and didn't realize so much time had passed. Come. Wash up, while I dish up our supper."

In the kitchen, Cal smiled at her, taking up the bar of soap and filling the basin with water. He washed his hands and face, glancing into the small mirror that hung above the washbasin, then dried his face and hands. I'm looking old, he thought, noticing how many more strands of gray hair were at his temples and in a shock at the front of his head. He ran a hand through it, then turned, going to his place at the table.

As they ate, they talked quietly of the day's events. "I had a visitor at the Mercantile today," Cal said. "A strange little man from South Carolina. He said he was a...let's see, how did he put it?...a *purveyor* of hopes and dreams, I think it was. I must have looked dumbfounded because then he explained he's a lawyer. He asked me where he could find lodging and a meal and I sent him over to the boardinghouse. A funny little man...seemed to be interested when I told him my name. Repeated it, and then said he'd see me later." He took a second biscuit, slathering butter on it, then glanced at Ophelia. He was surprised to see her staring at her plate of untouched stew, grimacing. "What is it?" he asked. "Ophelia? What's wrong?"

To his surprise, she rose, hurriedly, covering her mouth with her hand, and rushed from the room. He set his fork aside and stood, not certain what had upset her, wondering what to do. Only once before in his life had a woman rushed away like that. Lea. But he had caused her to. Had something he said *this time*, too, caused Ophelia to hurry away? He listened to the sounds of the house: the murmurs of patients and their visitors, then coughing, followed by someone moaning, and then more coughing, and suddenly—his thoughts drifting—he felt terribly tired. If only things had been different, he thought. I'd be in that house I always planned to build out on my property. Lea and I would be there. *Lea...it still* came back to Lea.

He walked from the kitchen, stretching as he went, then slowly climbed the stairs to his bedroom. For just a moment, thoughts came of the little man who had entered his store earlier that day. Cornelius, he'd said his name was, Cornelius T. Attbury, a *purveyor* of dreams. Cal laughed softly. Some dreams even a purveyor couldn't make come true. Some dreams...his thoughts drifted off. He knew better than to let himself think of Lea. How many times had this same sense of loss governed his mood when she came to mind? He was too smart a man to chase a dead dream. He'd be better off counting his blessings like the minister had preached in church last Sunday. Didn't he have a wife that loved him? A good wife, loving and sweet. A wife who gave to him in ways far beyond his expectations, all the warmth, love and comfort *any* woman could give. Why couldn't that be enough? Why couldn't *she* be enough? He was happy, wasn't he? Happy and well pleasured. What more could a man ask? He shook his head in disgust at himself. I'm an old man now, but an old man that lacks a certain peace of mind. Regrets trouble me...regrets I can do nothing about. For a moment, to his surprise, he thought of Sarah Gentry. He had been so taken with her after Lea left. A beautiful woman she was. Not Lea, but a most desirable woman. A woman who had married his best friend, Moses.

Funny, he thought, how life has a way of holding so much promise. Then, just as we reach for it, bang! Something comes along to change things. He took a deep breath, wondering how Sarah was, having no idea she had met her death, a few weeks before, at the hands of a cavalry officer who had led an attack on the Lakota village. He wondered if Sarah had ever regretted leaving to live among the Indians? He doubted it. Then, his thoughts drifting, he said aloud: "And much as I wish it, I doubt my sweet Lea will *ever* return." From the doorway there came a small gasp. Ophelia stood there, staring at him, having heard his every word.

CHAPTER 6

Ophelia turned and raced down the stairs as fast as she was able, hearing the sound of Cal close behind. She rushed through the kitchen and out the back door, the cold wind a shock as it buffeted her body. She wore no coat, and the snow quickly covered her, though she paid it no heed. She wanted only to run and run, until she managed to disappear into its thick white embrace and hide. Hide from Cal, and the grief he had caused her as she heard the words he had spoken. Words that tore at her heart, rendering it as cold as her snow-blanketed surroundings. She slipped, nearly falling, and realized tears—like tiny pieces of ice—lay upon her cheeks. Panting, she slowed to catch her breath, and felt Cal's hand close upon her arm.

"Leave me alone," she cried, turning toward him, not able to help noticing how cold he looked, his dark hair already all but hidden beneath a thick coat of snow.

"Ophelia, I'm sorry," he said, trying to pull her close and wrap his arms around her to warm her. "Come back to the house. You'll catch your death out here."

"Why do *you* care?" she shouted above the hollowing wind. "It would free you. That's what you want, isn't it?" she cried, and she began to shiver as much from the sadness she felt, as from the cold.

"We have to go in, Ophelia. We'll talk when we get inside. Oh, honey, I'm so sorry," Cal said, trying to console her. Even though the heavy shirt he wore—a shirt Ophelia had made for him—he was shaking badly from the cold, and he knew her dress was much thinner. It was imperative he get her inside as quickly as possible. In one swift and unexpected movement, he reached out, lifting her up into his arms, and gathering her to him. He turned, intending to carry her back to the warmth of the house, feeling how badly she was shivering. Still she tried to twist free of him, but it was no use. Then, without warning, she slumped against him, no longer struggling...or caring.

Winded, Cal shoved open the door, thankful to feel the heat inside the kitchen. He kicked a chair away from the table and sat Ophelia down on it, grabbing a nearby towel and began drying her hair. Startled by her lack of response, he moved quickly, feeling both worry and fear. She sat there, staring at the floor, her eyes showing the tremendous pain he had caused her. Grabbing his coat from where it hung by the door, he placed it around her shoulders, then bent to take off her shoes, knowing her feet had to be as cold as his felt. He rubbed her feet briskly between his hands, trying his best to warm them, and was painfully aware of her silence. How can I make her understand? he thought. How can I *ever* make amends? Will she ever believe how sorry I am, knowing my feelings for Lea still exist? He continued to rub Ophelia's feet, more than a little aware that she avoided all eye contact. He wanted to tell her what he felt, wanted to tell her how sorry he was, but this was not the place, nor the time. When they were upstairs alone, then he would tell her how much he cared for her. If only she hadn't heard me, he thought, and he shivered, realizing how cold he was, too. But it was no match for the coldness in her eyes.

"Ophelia, let's go upstairs, honey. Come on," Cal spoke softly, reaching up to take his coat from her shoulders. Then he took both her hands in his, noticing that she offered no resistance. It was as if the life had gone out of her, and it devastated him to see how badly he had hurt her.

"What's going on?" Aunt Hilda asked, bustling into the kitchen, the broom in her hands. She glanced from Ophelia to Cal and back again, knowing by the looks on both their faces that something was dreadfully wrong. She paused to lean the broom against the cupboard, then placed her hands on her hips, and faced Cal. "I asked a question," she said, her voice firm. It was evident she expected an answer and would not leave without one.

Cal cleared his throat. "It's...between Ophelia and me," he replied, knowing that answer would not satisfy her.

"I see," stated Aunt Hilda, and he could see her jaw tighten, and knew she would not let it pass. She stepped around him, picking up a large kettle and quickly filled it with water. Setting it on the stove to heat, she turned back to face him, her chiseled features reminding him of an old warrior about to do battle. "I saw Ophelia running through the snow, running from *you*. You may think it's between you and my niece," she stated, firmly, "but if it concerns my niece, it *is* my business. I'm *making it* my business."

Cal cleared his throat again, obviously nervous. "Right now, it's more important we get her out of these wet clothes," he stated. "You can make it your business, once Ophelia is warm, *not before*."

Aunt Hilda was taken aback by Cal's answer, having never seen this side of him. And he was right, she had to admit that. She moved to the stove, testing the water to make sure it wasn't too hot, then got out the basin from under the stove and poured some of the water into it. "Put your feet in this warm water, Ophelia," she said, "they're practically blue from the cold. What were you thinking? Why would you run outside in such terrible weather?" Ophelia sat still, not answering, and Cal bent to lift her feet, one at a time, and place them into the basin.

Aunt Hilda picked up the towel and began trying to dry Ophelia's hair, just as Auntie Belle came into the kitchen.

"Well, what's going on?" Auntie Belle asked, smiling her usual happy smile. She looked from Cal to Ophelia to Aunt Hilda, each one of them looking more solemn than the other. She waited, but no one answered. Seeing that Ophelia's dress was wet clear to her knees, and her hair was also wet, she couldn't help wondering what was going on. She, too, had happened to pass by a window just as Ophelia ran out of the house, with Cal not far behind. "It's much too cold a day, Ophelia, to be running around in the snow like a frisky colt," she said, trying, as usual, to lighten the mood.

"Oh, shut up!" both Aunt Hilda and Cal said, at the same time.

Auntie Belle's mouth dropped open in surprise. She was used to her sister talking to her like that, but never Cal, and it hurt her more than words could tell. She glanced at the floor, and felt her cheeks turn red with embarrassment, then turned on her heel, nearly running down Father Patrick as he came around the corner.

"Hello, folks. Terrible weather we're having. Why, what's going on?" Father Patrick asked as he quickly side-stepped to keep from being run down by one aunt, and found himself staring into the glaring eyes of another. Cal, on the other hand, looked like he wanted to crawl under the table and hide. Patrick's gaze then fell to Ophelia. "Has something happened?" he asked. "Can I be of any help?" Cal groaned, hanging his head, and Aunt Hilda snorted, loudly. Father Patrick cleared his throat, realizing his presence seemed to be more of a hindrance than a help, and nodding toward Ophelia—the only one who *wasn't* looking at him—he backed out of the room and went to find Auntie Belle. It looked as if she was crying as she rushed past him, and he knew it would take a lot to make her cry. She might not need him in a priestly capacity, but it looked certain that his favorite aunt needed a friend, and he couldn't pass up such an opportunity. How many times, in all the years he'd known her, had he bared his soul to her over a morning cup of tea or coffee? How many times had she listened patiently as he read his sermons to her, glad to have her comments and advice? He wasn't her priest, but he was her friend, and he hoped just maybe he could put a smile back on her face.

In the kitchen, Cal saw Ophelia shiver, then straighten up in the chair. He glanced up, seeing that Aunt Hilda was also watching her, and she took a deep breath before asking, "Ophelia, I saw you run out into the snow. Why, land sakes, child, you know better..."

"I'm fine, Aunt," Ophelia said, so quietly that Cal wasn't sure she had spoken, at first. "I need to get baking for our patients," she said, pulling her feet from the basin of water that had begun to cool. "If you'll hand me the towel, please," she said to Cal, not looking up at him. He handed it to her, wishing she would look at him.

Well, I don't know what you were thinking," Aunt Hilda said, snorting softly and shaking her head. "If your husband..." she began, but Ophelia cut her off before she could say more.

"Aunt, please. It'll be all right." She rose from her chair, still shivering, and brushed a few strands of damp hair back from her face. Then she reached forward, giving her aunt a quick kiss on her cheek, slipped past her, and quickly headed upstairs to change out of her wet clothes.

Aunt Hilda watched her go, then turned toward Cal, but he rushed around her and dashed up the stairs before she could say a word. She stood there, thoughts flashing back to the day she'd learned that Ophelia's mother had been beaten to death by her father while he was in one of his drunken rages. She hadn't been there to protect her sister, hadn't even heard of her death until days later. She looked down at the floor, noticing the water that had splashed there. No man, she vowed, drunk or not, would *ever* hurt her nieces. She hadn't seen any marks on Ophelia, and didn't know what had driven her out into the storm without her coat or hat. But one thing she did know; Ophelia had been running from Cal, that was as plain as day, and that was all she needed to know. If he ever dares to hurt her, Aunt Hilda thought, it'll be over *my* dead body, and that's a promise. "Yes, sir," she said aloud, "that's a promise, *Mister* Dunnevey. You can count on it!"

Ophelia walked to the wardrobe in the corner of their bedroom, opening it and taking out one of her everyday dresses. It wasn't as pretty as the one she'd had on, but what did it matter, she thought. She heard Cal come into the room, but ignored him, going about the business of changing out of the wet dress, her back to him. She heard him clear his throat as if he was about to speak, but silence prevailed. Stepping out of her wet dress, she kept her back to him, careful not to let him see the slight bulge of her belly. But thoughts of the baby she was certain she was carrying made her eyes fill with tears. Why now? She thought. He still wanted *Lea*, not *her*, and certainly not this baby. She sniffled, noticing some tears had fallen onto the dress she now wore. Hanging the wet dress to dry on a hook near the wardrobe, she turned, ignoring Cal, who sat slumped in a chair across from their bed. Walking to the small table that stood next to the bed, she picked up her brush and began brushing her hair, hoping for the first time, that she wouldn't catch cold from her dash out into the snow. It had been a foolish thing to do, she was well aware of that. An especially foolish thing for a respectable woman her age to do, but his words...she shook her head, trying to erase from memory what she'd heard him say. Lea, she thought, *always Lea*, and thoughts of her sister brought fresh tears to her eyes. Laying the brush back on the table, she covered her face with her hands, unable to stop herself from crying as her heart broke anew.

CHAPTER 7

When Ophelia started to sob, Cal felt even more ashamed than ever. If only she hadn't heard, he thought. If only I could take it back, tell her she'd misunderstood. Tell her I didn't mean it. But it was too late for that, he knew that. He rose and walked to their bed where she sat crying. Kneeling down in front of her, he eased his arms around her, wondering if she'd push him away, or scream at him to leave her alone, like she'd done outside. To his surprise, however, she didn't stop him, or shout at him. She simply continued to cry. He wrapped his arms around her, laying his head against her shoulder, his shame immense. I've never hurt a woman before—except for Lea—he thought, and he shook his head, sadly, ashamed that *even now*—with his arms holding Ophelia, *Lea* had crept back into his thoughts. He pulled Ophelia closer, feeling the dampness of her tears on his cheek, and whispered how sorry he was, that he'd never meant to hurt her, never meant for her to hear. Hadn't they had a good marriage? Hadn't they been happy together? Could she, would she *ever* forgive him? She gave no answer. And though her sobbing had turned to soft whimpers, she still shivered within his arms, and he wondered if it was because of how badly he'd hurt her, or that she'd taken a chill. If only I'd kept my thoughts to myself, he thought. I didn't mean to hurt her. I didn't know she was standing there, listening. He loosed his hold on her and began rubbing her back, whispering again how sorry he was, asking her to look at him, to believe him. He felt her shudder, then lift her head, her hands no longer covering her face. Looking into her eyes, he doubted she would *ever* forgive him, and he felt sick at heart.

"I need to see to my patients," she said, her voice a mere whisper, as she wiped the tears from her cheeks.

"Ophelia, please. I'm so sorry," he said, not wanting her to go. "If only I..." he began, but she closed her eyes, taking a deep breath, then gently pushed his arms from around her.

Standing, he knew it was no use to say more. She had always been aware of how he felt about Lea, he hadn't made a secret of it. Why should a few words make such a big difference? It wasn't as if he *meant* her to hear them, was it? Guilt and remorse made such thoughts abound, and he stepped back, watching her straighten her skirt and stand, then turn and go slowly down the stairs. He made no further attempt to stop her. It would do no good, and he knew it. Did she expect him to chase after her? No, not Ophelia, he thought. Ophelia was strong. She'd get over it. Why, by tomorrow morning she'd probably forgive him and be her usual sweet-natured self. She was right to get back to work. She had a duty to her patients. Why even Doc counted on her. Look at how much time she spent nursing *me* back to health, when I was her patient, Cal thought, and thinking that made him feel more ashamed than ever.

He remembered how she had come to his room each morning, her voice soft when she spoke, and always so cheery. He thought of how she had scolded her aunts when they had attempted to feed him, telling them he was a man, an adult, and he did not need to be babied...these thoughts cut into him, not easing his conscience, but intensifying his regret.

He walked over to the window, staring out at the thickly falling snow, a great sadness filling him. As he stood there, he saw in his mind the evening she had come to the Mercantile to tell him she intended to make Johnathon's grand home into a hospital. She'd been afraid he would laugh at her, he remembered, and when he hadn't, he remembered how happy she'd been. So happy, in fact, that she had leaned over and kissed him, and how surprised he'd been, not able to see it coming because of his blindness. He smiled as he remembered how totally unexpected it had been, how impulsive on her part, and how pleased he had been when he thought about it after she had left.

He raised his hands to his head, shaking it slowly back and forth. Whata fool I am, he thought. She had asked him to move that night, to live here, with her. It had shocked him when she asked, yes, but still she had asked, telling him she was so afraid he'd be offended by it. And he wasn't, really. He was quite flattered, in fact, but knew the damage such a move could do to her reputation. A woman, unmarried, living in a house with an unmarried man. Oh, how tongues would have wagged! He smiled as he thought this, yet just as quickly his thoughts sobered. He remembered the day he'd realized something was missing from his life. His sight was partially back, yellow-toned, but back enough that he could make out shapes and movement. He was laying on his bed, trying to figure out what it was he was missing, going over and over in his mind why he felt so...so...empty and alone, and suddenly he'd had this vision of Ophelia in his head. Ophelia, bending over him, her hand light upon his arm, asking if he needed anything, if she could get anything for him, if he was comfortable. That was when he had realized that *she* was what he was missing, she had become a necessary part of his life, a missing part of ...*him.*

Cal groaned aloud at this thought. It wasn't Lea who had stayed, no matter what he'd said or done. It wasn't Lea who had tended him, night and day, never failing to try to cheer him. Nor was it Lea who helped him shave, who cared if he was lonely, or scared, or...who cared if he was afraid...or cared if...or...*cared.*

"Dear God, what a fool I've been," Cal whispered, glancing around the room. "What an absolute jackass!" With those words left hanging in the air, he turned and raced down the stairs, shouting Ophelia's name.

Finding the kitchen empty, he raced down the hall, surprising the visitors from one of the rooms, as he nearly collided with them as they were leaving. Rushing on, he tore into the parlor, coming face to face— to his dismay—with Aunt Hilda. "Where is she?" he asked, then turned before she could answer, and bolted for the room he used to stay in as a patient; the room nearest the front door.

Aunt Hilda bit her lip, having seen the look on his face, then turned back to her dusting. A lover's quarrel, she thought, that's what it had been. Just a lover's quarrel that would soon be all made up, by the looks of it. If she was any judge of men, that is. She smiled, shaking her head. "Well, I hope she humbles him a bit, before she forgives him. That'll serve him right. But he won't get off that easy from *me*. The nerve of him, raising his voice to a nice old lady whose only intention was in protecting her flesh and blood...not to mention, him also telling my sister to shut up! Well, we'll see just how soon these sisters forgive you, *Mister Dunnevey.* We'll just see." And she stuck her nose in the air, sniffling loudly to show her disdain for him.

Auntie Belle sat in the parlor, sniffling into her handkerchief. Father Patrick sat across from her, his eyes filled with concern. How ashamed she felt to think that Cal, of all people, had spoken to her in such a manner, telling her to shut up, of all things. Thinking of it, her eyes again filled with tears. She was used to her sister speaking to her like that. Annathea had always been bossy and rude. It was something she had gotten used to over the years. Being the eldest, she'd gotten in the habit of bossing me, Auntie Belle thought. I never really minded, always accepted it as my due. Father always said she had more sense than I had, after all. He'd said that as far back as I can remember, and well, he seemed to be right. She always did better in school, got her lessons done much quicker than I. And her answers were always—or almost always—correct, whereas mine were...not. She sniffled again, glancing over at the young priest, seeing the kindness and compassion on his face. He was such a special fellow, her friend from the first day they'd met. She smiled a slight smile, noticing the wisps of red hair that stood straight up at the back of his head, and the freckles that dotted his cheeks and nose. Such a dear, dear friend, she thought, and as she thought it, he reached over and patted her hand, then turned to watch the fire in the fireplace. He didn't say anything, and she was glad, knowing that when he did speak it would be words well worth hearing. He might be young, she thought, but she'd heard about all the miracles that happened when he was around. Why, just the other day she had run into Juliana in the Mercantile, and they'd gotten to talking about him. Juliana had told her how he had ridden down the hill, right into that group of savages that had killed her family. Told her he'd been reciting the Mass, of all things, and the Indians had turned heel as fast as all git out and rode off as if the devil, himself, was after them. Auntie Belle would have liked to have heard more, but just then Juliana's grandfather, Jacob Wright, had entered the store and asked Juliana if we ladies would care to join him for a cup of tea at the boardinghouse across the street. She sniffled again, her cheeks reddening slightly at the memory.

Jacob Wright was a big man with flowing white beard and blue eyes that seemed to twinkle when he laughed. He laughed easily now, but that had not been the case, of course, when Auntie Belle had first seen him at the hospital. She remembered how they had found him, thin and worn, laying unconscious on the parlor floor in front of the fireplace. It was bad enough that he hadn't eaten in who knows how long, when they'd discovered him there. But the losses he had suffered were even worse: the loss of his beloved wife of forty-some years, and their daughter and her husband: Juliana's parents. How he'd survived the Indian attack, she didn't know. But the shock of what he'd been through had brought about his loss of memory, and she shook her head, remembering how he'd cried out his wife's name, when his memory began to return. Her name had been Juliana, Auntie Belle remembered; the name given also to their oldest granddaughter. Now Juliana, her little sister, Mary, their two brothers, and Jacob were settled in a small cabin out on Old Mill Road, just a stone's throw from Jonas and Lilly Hart's place. The small cabin, a rickety shed, and land they stood on, belonged to Jonas and Lilly. Jonas had offered it to them out of the goodness of his heart, when he heard what they'd been through. The first week, thanks to Jacob, the door no longer sagged, the window had been repaired, and the fireplace no longer filled the cabin with smoke when a fire was built. Jacob seemed able to do just about everything, including building, though the fact that his memory still had not totally returned caused him untold frustration, Juliana had confided to Auntie Belle. Juliana tried to fill in the gaps for him, but he said it was as if she was merely telling him a story of someone else's life, not his own. He just could not seem to connect the events she described, with *him*, having no feelings about them. He had been a farmer, building things of wood in the evening, after he'd finished chores. Sitting before the fireplace, his work-worn hands holding his knife in a deliberate manner, he'd carved his wife a fine shelf for her kitchen, and another for their bedroom, Juliana told him, hoping to jar his memory. He had listened attentively, she told Auntie Belle, then shook his head, sadly, and gathering up his pipe, walked out onto the porch. Juliana felt sad, knowing all she had said had not helped him remember, she said, and her eyes had filled with tears as she talked.

Now, only weeks later, Jacob—with much help from the Harts' and the other good folks of Hastings—had not only the loan of a cow, to provide milk, butter, and cheese for the children and himself, but sturdy chairs, a table, and two beds with comfortable straw mattresses, two oil lamps, six warm quilts, clothing, shoes for each of them, and all the food they needed until they could get on their feet come spring. A standing account at both the Mercantile and the German family's store provided all else they required, and Jacob could not believe the kindness shown to him and his family by folks in Hastings. Though they were complete strangers, the people of Hastings had gone out of their way to show them a bounty of Christian kindness he had never expected. He had walked through town that first week, introducing himself and shaking hands with the merchants, giving them his word that he would repay their many kindnesses just as soon as he was able. His hat in his hand, he had stood during Sunday services at the little church, asking to speak, if he may. Everyone had turned to face him, smiling at the four children that huddled close to him, glancing up shyly, their hair combed, and clothing—mostly too large—clean. "I'm Jacob Wright," he said, clearing his throat. "And these here are my grandchildren: Juliana, Mary Jo, Jared, and James. Stop fidgetting, James. Most of you know what the children and I have been through, and...well...I wanted to take this time to thank each one of you for the help you've given us. I...I still don't have much of my memory back; it comes and goes, a little each day."

"That seems to be the way of it for all of us older folk," a man stated, from one of the pews in the back of the church, and everyone laughed, nodding their heads in agreement.

"Anyway, I just wanted you to know that we're grateful for your many kindnesses, and will do our best to repay each and every one who has helped us, as soon as we're able. Thank you." With that, clapping filled the room, and men closest reached out to shake Jacob's hand, or patted him on the shoulder. One of the ladies winked at Mary, and a little boy sitting in front of them stuck out his tongue, causing his mother to whisper something in his ear that made him quickly turn and face forward, his face becoming so red that even his ears looked afire.

"I think I speak for all the folks of Hastings—or at least for the ones in church this grand and glorious morning—when I say welcome to our town *and* our church, Jacob Wright. It's a pleasure to have you and your young'uns here with us," the preacher said, adding, "and now shall we sing my favorite hymn, "Rock of Ages.""

Auntie Belle had been in church that Sunday, sitting not far from the Wrights, and she thought it a fine thing Mister Wright had done, and a brave one, too, she supposed, standing up in front of a whole bunch of strangers like that, and thanking them. She was bursting with admiration by the time she got home. Removing her coat and boots, she had hurried to tell Aunt Hilda every detail. Always one to dampen her spirits, Aunt Hilda had been quick to say that she would have to meet this Mister Wright. Auntie Belle was surprised by this and asked, "Well, whatever for?"

It took her aback, when her sister replied, "Why, he might just be needing a *wife* before long, sister. That's why. With all those young children under foot, it would take a strong, hard-working woman like *myself* to take charge."

"Are you all right?" Father Patrick asked, noticing the forlorn look that had suddenly appeared on Auntie Belle's face.

She jumped when he spoke, having been lost in thought, not even realizing he was still sitting quietly near her. "Oh, Father!" she exclaimed. "I was a million miles away in thought. I'm sorry." She sniffled, then blew her nose and wiped her eyes. Shaking her head, she looked over at the young priest, a questioning look in her eyes.

"What is it?" he asked, smiling at her.

"How do you do it? How do you just sit and watch all the others go about their lives?"

"I don't know what you mean," Patrick replied, questioningly. "Doesn't it seem unfair, somehow, that all the others got wives, Father, and children, and...well...here you are; young and not an ugly man, and you...you know...you're missing all that: a family of your own and place of your own. It doesn't seem fair, somehow. All these years I've done the same; watched the others marry and soon raise fine families, become parents and then grandparents, and sometimes I felt like life was passing me by. Do you know what I mean? Like I'd *missed* my chance for all that. I don't want to die alone, Father. Do you understand? But I'm already old, *too old* for all that, it seems. I don't mean to complain. I love helping the folks who come into the hospital; tending their needs, cheering them a bit if I can, bringing them a cup of coffee, or some comforting words.. .1 know the Lord is pleased when I do that. But, sometimes—and I don't mean to sound ungrateful— sometimes I think as how *I'd* like all that other...a good man to care for me, and a whole bunch of children to love, who would love me back. You know?" She sighed deeply, turning to look out the window, an old woman with dreams she hoped were still to be had.

Father Patrick reached out, taking her hand within his. "I know exactly what you mean. I understand those times...when it seems that all the love and laughter of family...are beyond reach. It doesn't matter what age you are, or what you do. We all have such longings. God made man and woman to become one, to marry and have children." He paused, gazing out into the storm that blew, coating everything in white, still holding her hand. "I always knew I wanted to be a priest. I never questioned it. But I knew the things of man that I would have to give up. It seemed hard, at first, being a young lad and all. Just like you, dear Belle, I'd see the other lads all gussied up, going courting, and I'd wonder if I was...you know...strong enough to answer the call of God. I'd wonder if I was good enough to forgo the things He asked of me, knowing He wasn't askin' it to cause me pain or sadness, but so I could better serve Him, putting none before Him, not even a wife." Patrick paused. He squeezed her hand, then let go of it, rising to go and stand by the fireplace. "I believe with all my heart that God has a

41

plan for each one of us, Belle. I believe with *all my heart* that He hears *and answers* our every prayer. Maybe not always as we wish them to be answered, but in His own wondrous way, knowing what we need to fulfill His plans for us." He turned toward her, smiling a smile that she would always think of as the smile of an angel. *"Pray* for the desires of your heart, Belle, and trust that He *will* answer. Until He does, take comfort in the wonderful outpouring of love and joy you bring to so many others, my friend."

Auntie Belle rose from her chair, seeing the faint glow that suddenly seemed to surround the young priest. She saw the way his eyes held hers; as if he was looking at her, but not seeing her. It was exactly like the look Juliana had described, when he rode down the hill and saved her and her younger siblings from the Pawnee. "Father..." Auntie Belle said, reaching out, touching his arm. "God bless you, Father." And as she said it, she saw the tears that glistened in his eyes, and knew she had witnessed something *so special,* that there *were* no words to describe it.

CHAPTER 8

Colin O'Leary pulled on his socks and boots, dreading the cold walk to the barn. He hated the cold more with each passing year. But chores had to be done; the cow milked and fed, the barn mucked out, and his brother, James, seemed happy to leave it to him. Scholarly, that's what James was; always poking his nose into some book. While *I'm* not interested in sitting all day by the fire, lost in the scribblin's of someone I don't know, Colin thought. Reading's what got me into trouble in the first place, after all. Reading of the South. His mind eased back to a time long since gone, but not forgotten.

He envisioned magnolia trees, bursting with beauty, and lovely azaleas, their branches covered with delicate crimson blossoms. It was a paradise, as sure as any he could have imagined; a paradise rich with promise, and warm, gloriously warm. No need to bundle up to keep the chill from your bones. No frozen feet or fingers, no suffering the ills that came with winter, or struggling to make it through drifts sometimes more than waist high to tend your critters. No sir, there'd been none of that in the South. Why, he'd thought he was as near to heaven as a man could get when he was there. Colin shut his eyes, wishing to lose himself in the memories, if only for a moment. Yet these memories brought not only feelings of contentment and longing, but unbearable sadness. It was gone now, lost, all of it...all of *them*.

He had never expected his life to change so drastically, when he agreed to accompany his friend home to spend the holidays. Colin had met Garret Nathaniel Montague—"Monty"—to his many friends, many years earlier, when both were young. They'd become the very best of friends. More like *brothers*, Colin often thought, knowing he'd never felt as close to *any* of his brothers, with the exception of William, that is. To say Monty impressed Colin was a complete understatement. With his laid-back ways, his indefatigable spirit—always ready for fun or fights; whatever might come his way—and most of all, his illimitable enthusiasm for helping right wrongs, he was as near an opposite to the hard-working, more serious Colin. Neither petty in his feelings or conduct toward others, and admirably generous, Monty stood fast against those who cared little for the downtrodden and poor. Colin had often seen him give the coat off his back to someone less fortunate, then shiver in the cold, a silly grin upon his face. Colin shook his head sadly, choked by the sense of loss he felt. Unlike Colin, Monty had seemed *driven* to act and speak against the cruelty and injustice he saw in life. Colin's thoughts turned back to the time they had come upon a plantation overseer whipping a slave.

Monty had become enraged by the sight and jumped from his horse, grabbing the man, giving him a good thrashing, followed by a tongue-lashing. The man had been completely surprised by the whole episode and simply lay where he fell, not saying anything in rebuttal. The negro had given a slight nod of thanks as Monty stooped to pick his hat up off the ground, and got back on his horse. Colin had asked—after Monty had time to cool down a bit—how it was that he could tolerate the fact that there were slaves upon his *own* family's plantation. Monty had turned on him, an anger burning in his eyes, telling Colin that there were *some* slaves that *weren't* treated poorly. Some slave owners treated their slaves practically as good as they did their own family, he said, sounding highly irritated. Then he had spurred his horse into a trot, leaving Colin to his own thoughts.

Colin walked to the cupboard—getting down a cup—then went to the stove and poured himself a coffee. It was early and both his maw and James were still asleep. He liked mornings like this; when the sun was just beginning to break over the distant hills and a certain stillness prevailed. He added more wood to the fire, then pulled a chair out from the table and sat down, stretching his long legs out in front of him. Katie came to mind, as he did so, and he smiled without realizing it. Katie Yeager. Oh how happy he'd been the first time he'd seen her. She'd come to the hospital, entering the parlor where he sat waiting for his maw who was in visiting with his brother, Michael. A lovely gal she was, with golden ringlets and the sweetest of smiles. He'd been awestruck by her loveliness, and knew it was just a matter of time until he'd get up his nerve to ask if he might come calling. It was then he'd discovered that her father was the brash fellow who'd thrown him out of his store. He had embarrassed him, screaming at him that he didn't want 'his kind' in his store.

Colin shifted, taking up his cup, still feeling embarrassed by the incident. Because I'd fought for the South, Colin thought. All because I'd fought on the other side. He took a swallow, feeling the coffee's welcoming warmth. Well, it takes all kinds, he thought. Every man's got a right to do what he believes in. I wasn't the only one who chose as I did. He took in a deep breath, his thoughts drifting back, once more, to his arrival at Avian Plantation, Monty's home. Colin had been totally amazed, never expecting such boundless beauty as he saw all around them as they rode down the long lane leading to the house. On two sides, huge trees—different than those in Minnesota—dripped with moss so thick that it obliterated most of the sun, leaving only a modicum of bright golden rays poking through. The heat bore down on them, and he had welcomed it, he remembered.

Monty looked over at him as they rode in, smiling at the look of surprise upon his friend's face.

"Welcome to Avian Plantation," he said, his voice soft, a look of pride upon his face.

"Saints be, Monty. I had no idea," Colin replied, still awed by the beauty of their surroundings.

"You've seen nothing yet, my friend," Monty said, laughing, and spurred his horse into a gallop, Colin close behind.

The heavy wooden double front doors opened as they raced up, and an older woman, and man who closely resembled Monty, stepped outside. Smiles broke upon their faces as they recognized their son, and the man hurried down the steps, embracing him as he dismounted.

"Mother, Father, may I present my good friend, Colin O'Leary from Minnesota," Monty offered, nodding toward Colin.

"Colin, my mother, Joanna, and my father, Colonel Renee Montague."

"How do you do? I'm glad to make your acquaintance," Colin said, not used to using such fancy language, glad he knew how to speak in such company.

"Welcome to Avian, sir. Any friend of Garret's is a friend of ours. But let's not stand out here in the heat. Do come in. Tell us all about your travels, Garret. I hope it was not a difficult journey?" his father asked, motioning a servant to bring them a refreshing drink.

"Colin's never been any farther south than Pennsylvania, Father, so I insisted he come with me to Avian. Told him he had to see how we of the South live." Monty laughed, reaching up to take the drink a slim young negress brought to him on a silver tray. He sipped it, not thanking her or acknowledging her in the least. As she approached Colin, he stood, smiling at her as he took the glass from her. He was about to thank her, when he noticed the surprised looks upon both the Colonel's and his wife's faces. Instead he nodded slightly at the young woman and resumed his seat. Monty was grinning from ear to ear, having all he could do not to burst out laughing, Colin realized, and he felt like slugging him. Good manners were good manners, he thought, and it shouldn't matter the color of a person's skin. Yet at Avian that did not apply, and Colin realized he obviously had a lot to learn about the South, and especially concerning servants.

Their conversation resumed, with much embroidering on Monty's part about their meeting and subsequent adventures, and the lessons learned from them. Colin listened, enjoying the gentle banter between Monty and his parents. They were so unlike *his* parents, who had always struggled just to survive, and had little time to enjoy such gracious pleasantries. *Their* abounding love for each other showed itself in the efforts they put forth, working together, side-by-side.

Joanna Montague basked in her opulent surroundings. An elegantly dressed, slender woman, quite fragile looking, she smiled tenderly at her son, her hands folded in her lap, a quiet calmness to her features. It was more than obvious that she had not a care in the world. Or, if she did, that it was petty, in nature, Colin thought, and couldn't help but wish *his* mother's life could be as easy and worry-free, and richly blessed.

Renee Montague, Monty's father, was a portly man, with a quick smile and commanding presence. He possessed a confidence that Colin found highly impressive. Colin knew *his* father would have been found sorely lacking, by comparison. Though Monty's father appeared to lack the enthusiasm and zeal that showed in his son, it was obvious he was more conscientious and attentive to details than Monty. Listening to their conversation, Colin had no doubt that he scrutinized matters thoroughly before he made any decisions, and this thoroughness and responsibleness had attained and secured—both for himself and his family—their station in life. Colin felt he could learn much from him.

And you, sir, have you found our great state of South Carolina to your liking?" Joanna asked, speaking softly, drawing Colin from his reveries.

"Yes, Ma'am," Colin replied. "Indeed I have."

Monty's father rose from his chair. "I'm certain you would like to rest awhile now, after your journey. We shall dine at seven. That should give you plenty of time to refresh yourselves, and for Garret to show you around Avian. You'll find the grounds particularly beautiful this time of year, Colin. I hope you'll enjoy your stay with us. If there's anything you need, don't hesitate to let one of the servants know. Now, if you'll excuse us, my wife and I will take our leave."

Both Colin and Monty rose, and remained standing, until the elder Montagues had left the room. "Come," Monty then instructed. "I'll show you to your room. It's right down the hall from mine."

Colin drank the last of his coffee, realizing James was stirring in the back room. He heard him coughing, and knew he'd soon be up. It surprised him that his maw had not yet awakened. She was usually the first one up. Colin rose and put another log in the fire, his thoughts drifting back in time, once more.

He'd never meant to stay so long in the South. Had intended to head back home when the harvest came in that year. *That year,* he thought. 1858, it was. He never expected his whole life to change like it had that year. Yes, there'd been plenty of talk of war and plenty of unrest, that was true. But that was only *part* of the reason he had stayed, and certainly not the main reason. The *main* reason came when he attended a cotillion with Monty at a nearby plantation, and met his beautiful cousin, Gabrielle Duchene. "Gabby, as he came to call her, stole not only his breath away the moment he laid eyes on her, but in that very same moment, stole his heart, rendering him blind to the charms of all other women. Gabby was exquisite, from the tip of her dainty toes to the top of her raven hair that glistened where it lay against her alabaster shoulders. Colin was mesmerized by her beauty and stood staring, speechless and awe-struck at the mere sight of her. He knew, from that very first moment, that she would be his wife. All else was unimportant. Neither home, nor crops; nothing else mattered, except that he win her favor and her hand. He was a man besotted.

"Colin, Colin!" James called, an urgency to his voice.

"What is it?" Colin replied, no longer lost in thought. He stood, hurrying toward his brother's room, wondering what had happened. At the door to their mother's room, he saw James kneeling, their mother's limp body cradled within his arms. Colin hesitated only a moment at the sight. "What's wrong? What's happened?" he asked, but he already knew the way their maw's head fell back, and by the tears that showed on James' face, that whatever had happened, it was too late to help her. He reached out, taking his mother's lifeless body from James, who now braced himself against the wall, his shoulders shaking as more tears ran down his cheeks. Colin carried her to her bed, laying her on it as gently as if she was a baby, and felt his own tears begin to fall. When finally he gained control, he stood, covering his mother and closing her eyes, then walked over to where James still leaned against the wall. "Brother," he said, his voice breaking, "we need to let Patty and Michael know. I'11 go, you stay with Maw," and he clapped James on the shoulder in a feeble attempt to comfort him.

On the long ride into town, first to the church to tell Patrick, and then on the even longer ride to Michael's, the same thought rode with him...gone, all gone, *everyone* he had ever loved was now gone. And the faces of Gabby, Monty, his brother, William, his paw and now his maw filled his mind as clearly as if they rode with him.

CHAPTER 9

Folks came from near and far to pay their respects with word of Kathleen O'Leary's passing. Her sons, Michael, Colin, James and Father Patrick stood silently by, their cheeks often damp, accepting the condolences of their townfolk. Auntie Belle took it upon herself to see to it that there was food aplenty and that they ate, and Aunt Hilda saw to it the cabin was neat and tidy. Doc Valentine kept the fire going, bringing in wood from the porch when needed, and explaining when questioned that Miz O'Leary had simply passed due to age. Examining her earlier, he had been unable to find any other cause, though James had told him he found her laying next to her opened Bible, on the floor of her room.

Katie Yeager came as soon as she'd heard, seeing to anything that needed tending, that wasn't already being done by the aunts, and making sure that Colin, James and Patrick each had a bite to eat. Even the preacher from Old Mill Church came to pay his respects, as did Katie's mother and grandmother, the new people who lived in the house that had belonged to Rosie and Angus MacGregor, and later that day, Eli and Jonas Hart—his wife, Lilly, feeling too ill to make the journey. Lydia O'Leary, Michael's wife and Lilly's sister, hoped Lilly had not stayed away because of her. They had not been able to "mend fences," as the saying goes, and though it bothered Lydia greatly, she accepted it, hoping that someday the love they *both* felt for Eli would not stand between them.

As Auntie Belle put on another pot of coffee, she heard the door open and turned, surprised to see it was Jacob Wright and his grandchildren who had entered. He smiled at her, as Juliana helped the younger children out of their coats and ushered them over to the hearth to enjoy the warmth of the fire.

"Good day, Miz Belle," Jacob said, his eyes looking into hers a slight bit longer than normal, as if studying her.

"Good day, Mister Wright. How kind of you to come. The boys are in the other room, if you care to go in and pay your respects."

"Indeed I will," he replied, smiling at her in a way that pleased Auntie Belle. He hesitated then, asking, "But, if I may, I'd like a word with you, Miz Belle, later?" and Auntie Belle nodded, hoping she wasn't blushing. He turned then, apparently not noticing, and walked into the other room to speak to Miz O'Leary's sons.

"Well, what was *that* all about?" Aunt Hilda asked, her voice sounding querulous, as she walked over to stand beside her sister. "I hope you aren't going to make a *fool* of yourself, sister. Do you realize how red your cheeks are? They're positively *flaming*."

Auntie Belle felt all the joy she had felt quickly disappear, and turned away from her sister.

"Really, Dorothea, this is neither the *time,* nor the *place* to..." Aunt Hilda began, but to her surprise, Auntie Belle whirled around, taking her by the arm, and pulled her toward the door. "What are you doing?" Aunt Hilda asked, barely able to keep her voice down, she was so greatly surprised.

Once outside, Auntie Belle shut the door firmly behind them and then turned to face her sister, her face much redder than it had been. "I have had *enough*, Annathea. Enough of your nasty remarks and the cruel habit you have of *always* finding fault with *everything* I say and do! I want it to *stop!* Do you understand? I don't know what Jacob Wright wants to speak to me about, but plainly it's *me* he wants to talk to, and *none of your business!* And with that, Auntie Belle turned and hurried back inside.

Aunt Hilda stood where she was, unaware of the cold winds that blew, causing her to shiver and gooseflesh to appear on her arms. She had never expected such a lecture from, of all people, Dorothea, and was vexed beyond words because of it. Why, she thought, who do you think you are, sister, to speak to *me* in such a manner? *I'm the one* who has always been so kind to you, taking care of you, watching out for you. Who is it who always sees to it you don't make a fool of yourself? She realized a buckboard was approaching, and snorting her disgust, opened the door of the O'Leary's cabin and went back inside, being careful to avoid her sister.

When the door opened next, it was the Dunnevey's, Cal and Ophelia, who entered. Ophelia looked peaked and pale and was not her usual happy self, it was noticed. Stamping the snow from their boots, they nodded to those they saw, greeting their friends as they passed, intent on heading right in to where Miz O'Leary's body lay. Both aunts were concerned at sight of their niece, having only now noticed the pallor of her skin, and the way she held tightly to her husband's arm. It worried them greatly, and they wondered if it was the disagreement, days before, or whatever it was, that had given Ophelia cause to race from the house *and* Cal, dressed in nary a coat or hat. Perhaps, they both thought, she's coming down with a cold.

Auntie Belle bustled about, noticing that there was little left in the coffeepot. So intent on making more, it was a few minutes before she realized that Jacob Wright was standing nearby, watching her. She brushed a strand of hair back from her face, giving him a quick smile as she put the pot on to brew. "I'll only be a moment," she said, feeling her heart race a bit from the excitement she felt.

Take your time, dear lady," Jacob said, and he walked over to sit beside his grandchildren, noticing that they were enjoying plates of food. "Wipe your chin, Jared," he said, keeping his voice low. "Aren't you eating, Juliana?"

"I've already finished, Grandfather," the young woman replied, smiling at him. "Miz Belle brought us each a plate," she said, glancing over at Auntie Belle and smiling.

"A lovely lady," her Grandfather said, then cleared his throat before asking, "you like her, do you?"

"Oh yes," Juliana replied, surprised by him asking.

It was then that Auntie Belle approached, straightening her apron, her cheeks rosy red. "How are you doing, children? Would you care for more to eat, James...Jared? How about you, Mary?" she asked, not noticing the look on Jacob Wright's face. "At least let me get you something to drink," she said, and was about to turn and go get the pitcher of tea that sat on the cupboard, when Jacob reached out and placed his hand on her arm.

"No need to trouble yourself," he said. "Juliana can see to the children. Juliana, please get your brothers and sister a drink." And he motioned for Belle to take the chair beside him. Auntie Belle was so surprised—not to mention—pleased, that she immediately glanced over to where Aunt Hilda stood watching, a sullen look upon her face.

Why, thank you, sir," Auntie Belle whispered, feeling her face flush with joy."What is it you wish to speak with me about?"

It was Jacob Wright's turn to look a little flustered, as he cleared his throat, and also glanced toward Aunt Hilda, seeing how perturbed Belle's sister looked. His face reddened almost as red as Belle's, and once more he cleared his throat before speaking. "I...ah...I'm not sure just where to begin," he said, stammering.

"Well, it can't be all that bad, can it?" Auntie Belle asked, smiling sweetly. "Have I done something to offend you?"

"I..." Jacob replied, shifting in his chair and glancing over at her sister once more. Again he cleared his throat, "Perhaps this isn't the proper place to...ah...say what I intended," he said, pulling at his collar and looking uncomfortable.

"It is as good a place, I suppose, as any," Belle replied, sadly, convinced now that she had done something wrong. She hung her head, looking down at her hands, taking in a deep breath. Then, suddenly, without warning, she stood, saying, "I'm sorry, sir, for whatever it is that I've done," and turned quickly away. She rushed over to where her coat hung, grabbed it and hurried out the door.

It took Jacob Wright a moment to realize that his hesitation had upset Belle. The poor woman thinks I'm about to find fault with her, he thought, and telling Juliana he'd be right back, he bounded from the cabin, not taking the time to put on his coat. Through the snow that had continued to fall, he saw Dorothea hurrying toward a buggy, and barely able to keep his balance, he began to run, shouting her name. She stopped, hearing him, and then climbed up onto the buggy's seat, intent on heading for home. She'd had all the tongue-lashings she could take for one day, first from her sister, and now, obviously one *he* intended to give her, too. She felt tears trickle down her cheeks and wiped them away, just as Jacob reached the buggy.

"Don't go, Miz Belle. Wait. Please. Forgive me for upsetting you," he said, trying to catch his breath. "I was wrong to say anything today. A funeral's not the place. Can you forgive an old fool such impulsiveness, dear lady?"

Auntie Belle looked at him, no longer certain which one of them was the fool. There he stood, this stranger to Hastings, his hair and shoulders covered with snow, and he was apologizing to her? For what?

she wondered. "Do get in the buggy," she said, "before you catch your death," and she moved over as far as she could.

Jacob climbed up onto the seat beside her, shivering from the cold, blowing snow off his thick white beard as he did so. He squeezed in beside her, grabbing up the horsehair blanket and pulling it around his shoulders. Belle sat quietly, wondering if he'd lost his mind. What kind of man runs out in such a storm, just to tell a woman how she's upset him? She rubbed her hands together, trying to get them warm, then tucked them under her coat. "You may as well tell me what it is that I've done," she said, lifting her chin so she could look him straight in the eyes.

Jacob Wright looked over at her, a questioning look upon his face. "Dear lady, you've done nothing wrong. Quite the contrary. It's I who have given offense. Truly it is I," he said, shaking with cold.

"I don't understand," Auntie Belle said, reaching to pull the blanket further up around his shoulders.

"Even now, you try to see to my comfort, Jacob said, looking at Belle like no man had ever looked at her before. You see, my dear, I find myself tongue-tied, *not* because of anger, quite the contrary. It's because I...I wish to ask you..." again he hesitated. Miz Dorothea Blossom—Auntie Belle—I want to ask you to be my wife.

Auntie Belle's mouth fell open in surprise. Never in all her days had she expected Jacob Wright to propose to *her.* She looked at him, seeing this big bearded stranger shivering before her. His hair was wet with snow, and matted against his head, and a piece of food stuck in his beard just below his lips. His shirt was one someone had given him and fit him poorly, his hands, sporting cuts and scrapes, and dirty fingernails testified to the hard work he'd been doing at his cabin. Yet looking into his eyes she saw only the kindness in them. Aware of the many thoughtful things she'd seen him do, and having heard Juliana tell of how hard a worker he was, Auntie Belle reached over, resting her hand within his large one, in answer. A loud bellow of laughter burst from him, as he folded his hands around hers, warming them as surely as he warmed her heart. Then they stepped down from the buggy and hurried back into the O'Leary's cabin, before one or both caught their death.

CHAPTER 10

Change—whether for good or bad—is difficult for most folks. It takes a modicum of effort and adjustment, at the least, and tremendous effort and adjustment, at most. Change, even if expected, can rattle a person right down to their bones. Yet, expected or not, and good or bad, change is as inevitable as breathing. It comes—whether we want it or not—affecting everything—and everyone—in its path. And that winter, change came charging into Hastings with a fury!

It was just after Miz O'Leary was laid to rest beside her beloved husband that things began to happen: first, at the hospital in town, and not long after at the 0'Leary place.

Six days had gone by—gloriously peaceful days—Auntie Belle had to admit, since Miz O'Leary's funeral. Six days, since her sister had so much as looked her way or spoken to her. Oh, she'd weaken one of these days. It was inevitable. It wasn't like Aunt Hilda to forgo the chance to give her—or *anyone*, for that matter—her opinion on things. Why, she must be just about to burst, Auntie Belle thought, and she couldn't help giggling at the thought. Six days, Aunt Hilda had kept silent, fuming and fussing, obviously, but not saying a word to anyone. Six blessed days. And all because Jacob Wright has asked *me* to marry, Auntie Belle thought. *Me.* Not Hilda, or the widow Yeager, but *me*. Auntie Belle felt like dancing, she was filled with such an overwhelming feeling of happiness. It lifted her up as if on the wings of an angel.

How many years had she hoped and prayed for a family of her own, and a good man to care for her. True, Jacob didn't love her. She knew that. But he needed her; that was a fact. Needed her to watch over his grandchildren, to see to their needs, to cook and clean, mend and plant; needed her to do the many things a woman could do to make a house a home, to make them a family. She smiled, noticing her jaws ached slightly from having smiled so much the past six days. It didn't matter that he didn't love her. If the good Lord was willing, that would come in time. There were far more important things to worry about than something as silly as love. She'd need to start right in with sewing him some shirts that fit. A man shouldn't have to wear borrowed clothes that were ill-fitting. And there'd be plenty of socks and mits to knit for the children, and...happy thoughts filled her mind as she went about her daily chores at the hospital, hardly aware of what she was doing.

They had decided to marry at the church on Old Mill Road the week before Christmas. There was no reason to wait, after all, with his wife having been lost in the Pawnee raid, months before. True, it was customary to wait a year or so, out of respect for the deceased. But both Jacob and Auntie Belle had discussed the fact that the children had needs *now*, and to wait any longer was pure foolishness. Oh, she knew that once Aunt Hilda started talking to her again, she'd hear about it, *plenty*. But she was tired of her life as it was. Tired of tending the sick and dying. She wanted what she had always wanted: a family to care for and love. She wanted children at her knee in the evening, happy children, their laughter filling their home, stomachs full of food she'd cooked for them, their lessons studied around the hearth, and prayers said before they slept. Oh, how she wanted these things. She had always wanted them, and waiting was out of the question. And Jacob needed her, too. That frightened her a little, never having had a husband. But she'd muddle through, somehow. He'd already told her he'd stay in the boys' room nights, if she wished it. That he'd not expect her to... well...be a wife, *that* way. But—her face fire-red, she was sure—she'd told him she'd be a wife in *every* way, if he'd like, but that he'd have to teach her what was expected of her. By the time she'd finished saying that, his face had gotten nearly as red as hers, though it was hard to tell, with his beard so thick. She giggled aloud, thinking back to the talk they'd had when he'd asked her to sup with him at the boardinghouse a week after Miz O'Leary's funeral. He'd seemed so upset, she remembered, fidgeting something terrible. Finally, she had asked him what was wrong. Had he changed his mind about her? "I have *not*," he had answered, straight out, so loud that some of the other folks eating there had turned to look at them. Then he stammered and cleared his throat, as she knew him to do when he was nervous. Finally, he had whispered so only she could hear, "Will I need to shave my beard?"

Belle had nearly dropped her cup of tea at realizing *this* was what was upsetting him. She looked at him steadily, taking her time, sipping from her cup, then sat it down and—brazen as all git out—she reached across the table to take his hand, before speaking. "Mister Wright, I am an old woman, yet you have asked me to marry. I require neither a young husband, nor a clean-shaven one, to do so." To her surprise, he sighed loudly, then raised her hand to his lips and kissed it, *both* their faces quickly becoming as red as the cloth under their plates.

Arriving at the hospital that evening—on the arm of Jacob Wright—her heart bursting with happiness, she was surprised to find Aunt Hilda waiting for them. Her joy quickly changed to dread as she nodded at her sister, noticing the sour look upon her face.

"I'll have my say," Aunt Hilda said in greeting, giving them a haughty and most challenging look.

"I'm sure you will, sister," Auntie Belle answered, removing her coat and hat and handing them to Jacob to hang up. He cleared his throat while doing so, and Belle felt a wave of sympathy for him.

Settling themselves in front of the fireplace in the parlor, both Belle and Jacob had only a second to wait until Aunt Hilda spoke. "Well, I see you're determined to go through with this, Dorothea," she began, raising a hand to stop Auntie Belle from answering. "It's just like you, sister, to forget so easily your obligation to Ophelia and our patients. Also, your obligation to *me*. Obviously you do not mind, *in the least*, being slack in your responsibilities, though I'll admit I did not think it would go so far." Again she raised a hand, stopping any further rebuttal from either Belle or Jacob. "I feel it my duty, as your sister, to caution you against such marked neglect, though it's quite apparent you no longer care for my opinion. Instead, you shilly-shally around town, heedless of the tongues that wag, because of your *shameless* conduct. This man is a stranger, after all, and who knows what manner of man he is. It's apparent he lacks *all decency and respect* concerning his wife's passing; brazenly courting you in front of the *whole* town and giving no heed to the *proper* rules of conduct in such matters." She stopped to draw in a deep breath, shaking her head to emphasize her disgust.

Tears ran down Auntie Belle's cheeks at the cruel upbraiding, so shamed was she by her sister's words. And Jacob Wright gripped the arms of his chair, his face nearly purple with rage beneath his beard, his fingers white where they dug into the chair. He had all he could do to keep his temper at bay, as he gathered the words he felt it necessary to say in reply.

Then, before Aunt Hilda could say more, he stood, walking over to her chair. Glowering at her and bending so his face was mere inches from hers, he drew in a deep breath, saying, "*Enough*, woman. You've said enough. Do you understand me?" It took every ounce of will for him to keep his voice at a decent level. "Your sister may cower from you. Lord knows you've bossed her far more than is reasonable. But you know *nothing* of my wife, or the life we shared. You're a cold-hearted *harridan*, you are. *Jealous* of the happiness your sister will have under my roof, once she's free of you. Jealous, to be sure, and that's apparent to *everyone* who's seen how you treat her. It's because of the *kindness* I've seen in Dorothea toward not only my grandchildren, but *everyone* she meets, that I've asked her to be my wife. She has more kindness in one tiny finger than *you* have in your whole body. I have little to offer her, that is the truth. But I've a strong back and stronger faith, and if she'll have me, my grandchildren and I will be blessed by her presence in our lives. And I *will* do my best by her. You, on the other hand, are a harpy, as sure as can be, and it's sad to see the cruelty you've shown Belle. When we marry, you'll be welcome at our home, but *only* when you come to your senses and change your ways." Then he turned back to where Auntie Belle sat staring at him, her mouth open in surprise. She had never had *anyone* stand up for her before, not her father, or anyone, and it pleased her far more than words could tell. "Belle, I apologize for the strong things I've said to the sister you love. But I'm not a man to stand by and watch someone I care about take the brunt of such cruelty. Forgive me, please. And know that I'll let no one—*no one*—ever treat you in such a manner. And now I'll take my leave, as I don't like to be gone from the little ones for any length of time." Then, to her surprise, he bent and placed a kiss upon her forehead, turned and bid Aunt Hilda goodnight, took up his coat, and walked out the door.

Silence filled the parlor—a silence so strong that it seemed to pulse—until Auntie Belle realized it was her heart she felt pounding. She rose from her chair, walked over to her sister, quickly bent to place a kiss upon her cheek, then bid her goodnight, receiving no reply. Feeling happier than she had ever felt, in spite of it, she walked down the hall to her room, a radiant smile lighting her face.

And so it came to be, that Dorothea Blossom—Auntie Belle, to all her friends—found the love she had always hoped and prayed for. And the change it brought—not only into her life, but the lives of Jacob Wright and his grandchildren—was a blessing to behold. But it was *not* the *only* change to come to Hastings.

CHAPTER 11

Colin O'Leary stood at the grave of his mother, hat in hand, his thoughts unsettled. He'd gotten through the funeral, greeting those who came to pay their respects, though he could not remember now who all had come, or what was said. It was normal for those who grieved; their thoughts and feelings numbed by the intensity of their grief, and he was no exception.

James had sat staring out the window often, since, his many books laying beside his chair, unread. Michael, on the other hand, had cried and clung to Lydia, his eyes red. Grief was different for each of them, and though he was used to it—having seen death so often while at Andersonville—Colin felt shaken by it, the loss being his mother.

With his maw's passing, a change had come to all of them, but especially to Colin. No longer was there a reason to stay at their home. James was the one who liked being there, though he was ambivalent when it came to chores. Colin smiled as he thought this. James had been a teacher before the war, and his love of books might foster that interest again, Colin thought. James had finally gotten his health back, thanks to maw's tender care, and of all her sons, he was the one who'd had no desire to venture out into the world. He was a homebody, as surely as Colin was not, and Colin imagined the day would come when James would find a gal and settle down, raise himself a fine family, and ask nothing more of life. True, the only woman he'd ever seen or talked to since his return from the war was Katie, but there were other women in town. One of these days James was sure to meet one.

Colin shifted, noticing the gray bank of clouds to the west. Katie... he'd said few words to her of late. He was pleased at how she'd taken right over upon hearing of his maw's passing. She'd seemed right at home at their place; dishing up food for those who came to pay their respects, taking their coats, ushering them into the parlor and quieting the children who stayed near the fireplace in the kitchen. He remembered seeing how she had comforted James, patting his arm and speaking softly to him when he'd stood at the casket, so close to breaking down. And after, taking him a cup of tea and smiling up at him with such tenderness. She'd make a fine wife, there was no doubt about it, but still he could not bring himself to let her know of his feelings for her. Pulling his hat down upon his head, he turned and slowly began the walk down the hill toward the house, shivering, knowing he would welcome the warmth of a cup of coffee and the heat from the fireplace, and hoped James had thrown another log on the fire. He entered, shaking snow from his coat and stomping it off his boots. Hanging his coat on a nail near the door, he saw that James was not in his rocker over in the corner, and he was glad. He'd seen the buggy tracks leading from the barn and down the lane. Obviously, James had gone into town. Probably hankering for a new book to read, Colin thought. Or just plain tired of sitting, day after day, staring outside. It was about time he got out, took a ride, went to town. Or maybe he went to see Michael. Colin poured himself a cup of coffee, then sat at the table, enjoying the warmth and quiet of the cabin. The heat from the fire felt good, and as he sat there enjoying it, his thoughts turned back to the year 1858, and the night he'd met Gabrielle Duchene...

He hadn't wanted to go with Monty to the cotillion. There was a good chance, he remembered thinking, that he'd say or do something wrong, not knowing the customs of folks in the South. Look at how shocked Monty's parents had been, he thought, when I stood to show courtesy to that little gal that brought me a drink. Monty's folks hadn't said anything, of course, but he'd seen the stunned surprise on both their faces, made even worse by the mocking grin that Monty couldn't suppress. Colin felt his cheeks redden with embarrassment. There was so much I had to learn back then, he thought, taking a sip of coffee.

I stood out like a sore thumb, that was for sure. At least I had looked the part of a southern gentleman, having borrowed some fancy clothes from Monty. That had helped ease my nervousness, somewhat. He sat with eyes closed, remembering their arrival at the cotillion...

As the driver halted the horse in front of wide veranda steps, a servant met their carriage, holding the horses steady, as another opened the carriage door. Monty's father quickly stepped down from the carriage, then turned to offer a hand to his wife. Joanna smiled at him, then took the hand he offered, alighting gracefully. Waiting as Monty got out of the carriage, they could hear faint voices and music playing softly from inside the lovely old plantation home. I'd wondered what they would think of *my* home in Hastings, if they knew it was a simple cabin, not a magnificent home such as this one, and so many others I'd seen, the further south we'd traveled. Straightening, intent on looking a gentleman, I tried to hide how uncomfortable I felt. I had only been to three dances in my life: barn dances. A far sight different, to be sure, than this "grand cotillion," as Monty called it. Unsure of myself, I had hoped to find a quiet spot off to one side, from where I could simply watch the dancing and not have to participate. I was certain there'd be some ladies with mighty sore toes, if I danced.

Colin refilled his cup of coffee, setting it on the table, and then walked to the window. He gazed out across the yard, not seeing the snow that continued to fall, blocking out sight of the three graves on the hill; his brother, William's and his parents'. Instead, he saw again the elegance that greeted them, as he and Monty entered the ballroom. Lovely young ladies filled the large room, stealing glances at all those who entered, though shyly, from behind lacey fans. Their dresses accented not only their beauty—of which they had an abundance—Colin noted, but soothed the eye as if he'd walked into a field of beautiful flowers all the hues of a rainbow. Following Monty across the room, Colin could feel all eyes upon them, and wished only to find the safety of a quiet corner, and not draw attention to himself. He had definitely not been comfortable in such elegant surroundings, and had wondered what his maw would say, if she could see him. She would never have believed one of her young'uns would be dressed like a dandy, and the guest of such a magnificent place. Colin smiled as he remembered, and wished *now* that he *could* tell his maw about that night. He had never told her, had never told anyone. What could he tell? He grimaced. There'd been Gabrielle, and the short time they'd had together. And then there'd been Andersonville. After that, there'd been...nothing. Nothing at all, except the long ride back to Minnesota. The looks of those he passed as he rode into Hastings, and the loss...dear God, the loss. He shuddered, wishing...yet knew it was too late for wishing.

The sound of a buggy arriving brought Colin back to the present, ending his memories. Figuring it was James, he walked back to the table, picking up his cup of coffee, just as the door opened and James walked in. To Colin's surprise he was not alone. Katie entered behind him, still laughing gaily at something James had said. Handing James her coat, she headed over next to the fireplace, rubbing her hands together to warm them. As she passed Colin, she smiled and reached out to pat his arm, commenting on how cold it was outside. Colin returned her smile, glancing over at James, feeling suddenly uncomfortable. Should I leave? he wondered. Or stay and try to act as though...as though what?

he thought. I have no claim to Katie. I've never even asked her to take a ride, much less told her of my feelings for her. He cleared his throat, then offered her a cup of tea, if she liked, or coffee—there was some in the pot, he thought. But Katie declined, asking if they'd like her to cook something. She told them she wasn't the best cook, certainly not as good as...then grew silent, though they all knew she was about to say their maw. She stammered a soft apology, biting her lip, looking first at James, Colin noticed, then him.

"No need to apologize," James replied, walking to the cupboard to get her a cup. *"I'd* sure appreciate *anything* you might cook," he said. "Don't know about Colin, but I've been hankering for a good meal. Been thinking of heading up to the boardinghouse for one, in fact. Truth is, neither one of *us* can cook—anything *tasty*, that is.

Katie laughed, picking up their mother's apron and putting it on over her dress. "And I thought you missed my company," she teased. "But it was only a home-cooked meal you missed."

"I...ah...I have some work to do in the barn," Colin said, and he walked over and put on his coat, then pulled on his hat. Going out into the cold was the last thing he wanted to do, but it was apparent to him that James liked Katie, and he felt awkward being there; as if he was an intruder. He had no claim on her, after all. She was a pretty girl; easy on the eyes. And there sure wasn't anything wrong with his brother's eyes. Colin turned, looking at Katie as she began peeling potatoes, her blonde ringlets tied back with a ribbon that matched her dress. James sat in his rocker, a contented look upon his face. His book lay open across his lap, but instead of reading it, he, too, was looking at Katie, a look upon his face...like a man gazing at a vision, Colin thought, and he walked outside, shutting the door quickly behind him.

So that's how it is, he thought, shaking his head. I had no idea. James and Katie...why didn't I see it? He picked up the pitchfork and began mucking out one of the stalls in the barn, wondering why he hadn't noticed before. Was it Maw's passing that pulled them together, he wondered. He remembered again how Katie had patted James' arm and comforted him as he stood at the casket. Remembered, too, how she'd fixed him a plate of food, insisting he eat. He stood still, seeing it all so clearly, and understood. James had always been the gentlest of souls. Maw had tended him when he came back from the war, even though it was hard on her, her hands being all bent like they'd been. She'd fed him, almost like a babe, Colin remembered, until his health at last returned. It was the way she was. Colin knew that. She'd always taken care of her boys, no matter their age. And James had been sick when he got home from the war. Most of the men with him had died, he'd said, of dysentery or other ills. He was one of the lucky ones—all things considered—in that he had lived.

Colin rubbed his forehead. It was always that way. James always needed someone to care for him. Even when young he'd been the one who needed Maw to tend him. He was *frail*, that's what Maw said, Colin remembered, and even though it was Patrick who did crazy things and got hurt doing them—always breaking his bones—it was James who had the most severe colds and sicknesses. Colin went back to mucking out the stall, realizing for the first time just how different he and his brother, James, were. *He* was strong, always had been. He *never* got colds, or laid abed with one illness or another. *He* was the one who Maw had counted on to get things done around their place; to plow the field and put up fences, to fix the buggy and tend any difficult jobs that needed doing. And, he thought, I was the one who left. I'm the one who rode away when younger and never looked back. He stood still, understanding at last, why the place had looked so bad when he'd returned after the war. Patrick was gone then, doing what needed doing to become a priest, and William was dead. Michael...well...Michael had *always* looked out for *himself first*. James was all that was left to tend the place before the war. James, who was happier with his head in a book. James, who could sit all day long, studying something to teach his students. James, who wasn't strong, but was...scholarly.

Colin shook his head, a slight smile upon his face. James would make the perfect husband. Not *me,* he thought. I don't want to stay in one place. I want to see what's out there, over the mountains. That's why I couldn't tell Katie I liked her. Liking isn't enough for a marriage. Liking's only enough for...a friendship. Gabrielle was the only woman I ever loved, and I guess that's not gonna change. Colin leaned the pitchfork against the wall, feeling sure of himself for the first time in a long time. Maw's gone, he thought, and James has found a gal who'll make him a good wife. It's time for me to move on. A smile broke upon his face as a feeling of certainty filled him. Yes sir, he thought, there's a whole lot of country out there that's calling my name, and I'll welcome the change.

CHAPTER 12

Arriving home that night, Katie bid James goodnight, surprised when he bent and placed a quick kiss upon her cheek. Not expecting him to do so, she wondered if it was because he sensed the upset she'd felt when Colin had returned to the cabin, telling them that he'd made up his mind to leave. Colin said he'd been thinking about it a long time, and now that his mother was gone there was no good reason for him to stay. It had hurt her when he said that, but she'd busied herself washing the dishes and cleaning up after they'd finished eating, and hoped it didn't show. She wondered if it was because James showed her such attention; bringing her to the cabin, and teasing her about her cooking and all. She had hoped it was Colin coming to call, when she noticed their buggy pull up at her door. Had wished it was Colin who had done the teasing and shown such interest in all she had to say, but it was not. She took up her mending and sat before the hearth, reliving the evening, in thought. Colin had looked so surprised when she came in the door with James. She'd noticed the surprised look upon his face, couldn't help noticing it. He had smiled at her, the same sweet smile he'd given her when they had first met at the hospital. It had nearly melted her heart. He was so handsome. Tall, with a "devil may care" look to him, his features ruggedly handsome, his eyes piercingly dark. She had felt an immediate attraction to him. She took in a deep breath, remember-ing...He wasn't like James. James had a...a...quietness to him, an easy going nature. Colin, on the other hand, seemed dashing and daring, like a knight of old, or the pirate she had read of, long before, in a book her parents had forbade her to read. Yes, Colin had that very same manner, she thought, and she bit her lip, thinking this. Her father had warned her to stay away from him, and she wondered if—being a man—he, too, realized the attraction this might hold for a young, inexperienced woman, such as herself. She smiled, continuing her mending, her mind on Colin and not on the job at hand.She could see, in her mind's eye, Colin riding up to their cabin, and she, his wife, rushing from inside to greet him. He'd dismount quickly, and lift her up into his arms, kissing her, smiling down at her, telling her how he'd missed her, wanted her, loved her..

Katie sighed, regretfully, knowing now that it was not to be. He was leaving. The mountains were calling to him, he'd said, and she knew she wouldn't have been happy, leaving her mother or her home. As much as she wished it, she wasn't the type to head out for places unknown, facing who knows what? She was happy here, with family, and with the friends she'd made. I'm more like James, she thought, a soft smile forming as she thought of him. And he *is* handsome in his own way. Not dashing or daring, no, but gentle and sweet. A good man who enjoys quiet evenings at the family hearth; reading and studying. He'd been a teacher before the war, a good teacher, every-one said. And he *did* like her, that was obvious. If she had met him *first*, if she hadn't hoped for something...someone...more...she sighed again. I should be ashamed, she thought. It is far more important to find a good man to marry, a decent man who has the virtues necessary to be a kind and caring husband. A man who will be content with having a family, and will lead his children on a path of goodness and righteousness.

She put down her mending, brushing back a strand of hair that curled across her forehead. There are some men, she thought, made for storybooks. Men who are...meant to be knights and pirates. Men who seek a life of adventure. She thought of the wanted poster she'd seen hanging on the bulletin board outside their store, just the other day. It showed a picture of three outlaws, offering a huge reward for their capture: dead or alive. Outlaws, too, had that same daring to them, she thought, and surely weren't good husbands. No, unless I want to end up a lonely old maid, I'd better get over this foolishness and start appreciating what a good man like James O'Leary might offer. I *am* happy in his company, after all, and do like his pleasant ways and the intelligent conversations we've shared. And he does make me laugh.

She rose, walking over to stand at the window, looking out into the darkness of the night. Her father would have been so happy, knowing there was no longer any chance of her and Colin having a future. She shook her head, shivering as she looked at the snow upon the ground. Yes, she thought, father would be so pleased. He never would have understood this...longing I feel. The longing for...well, I don't know just what it is I long for. It isn't adventure, or heading out across some distant mountains, like Colin said *he* wanted to do. It's a longing for...she tried to put a name to it. Colin would have understood, she was sure.

She turned away from the window, sighing. Colin has the quality I'm longing for...a certain nature, she thought. A certain daring. She shook her head, biting her bottom lip, gently. She heard a buggy pass, then heard loud snoring from her grandmother's room, and knew that though she might long for something—or *someone*—who stirred these feelings inside of her, she was where she was meant to be. And if the good Lord favored it, she was certain He would lead James to want her for his wife. Of the few men she'd met in Hastings, James was the one she was most comfortable with. He had so many of the qualities she valued, when she wasn't thinking such foolish thoughts. It's obvious I need to set my mind on sensible things, she thought. I should have known a man like Colin O'Leary wouldn't stay. I should have known he'd ride away, seeking whatever it is that draws a man such as him. I should have known, she thought, and felt an overwhelming sense of sadness for what might have been.

CHAPTER 13

Ophelia Dunnevey walked down the hall to tend one of the children who had recently entered the hospital with a seriously high fever. There would be plenty of work to do; with every room of the hospital filled to capacity, and only her aunts to help with the feeding and cleaning, not to mention, tending to everyone's needs. She didn't know how long she could keep up the pace, noticing that every day she felt more and more weary. She hadn't expected to feel tired, but that must be part of being with child, she thought. And thinking of the baby within, she smiled, knowing that before long she would have to tell not only her aunts, but Cal.

Why she hadn't already told, she wasn't sure. The upset she'd felt when she had overheard Cal speaking about Lea was part of it, she supposed. And then there had been the funeral of Kathleen O'Leary to attend, and so many sick folks needing her care. I'll tell them tomorrow, she thought, smiling brightly as she entered the room of the newest patient. She was surprised to see a red rash all across the child's face and body, and began immediately to whisper words of comfort as she laid a cool wet cloth across his forehead. It was obvious, even before she touched him, that he was burning up with fever. The little boy looked up at her, his eyes glazed and sweat upon his brow. "It'll be all right," she whispered, shaking her head at seeing how feverish he was. "Don't be afraid, Ambrose. We'll get your fever down and you'll be back home in no time."

He looked at her with wide eyes, groaning as she removed the cloth that no longer felt cool, dipped it back in the basin of cold water, then placed it back across his forehead. "Sore throat, missus, the child squawked, his voice quivering as he spoke.

"Doc Valentine will be here in a few minutes. He'll give you something for your throat *and your* fever," Ophelia said, well aware that there were now five children in the hospital, all complaining of sore throats and suffering from high fevers. She hoped Doc would hurry. "Would you like a cold drink of water," she asked, and the boy nodded, giving a weak smile at her suggestion. "I'll be right back," she said, and she patted his arm tenderly, cooled the cloth again in the basin of cold water, and placed it back across his forehead. Then she turned, hurrying from the room.

As Ophelia neared the kitchen, she saw the surrounding walls begin to spin. Reaching out, she grasped at the wall as she felt her legs give way beneath her, and before she knew it she began to fall. She hit the floor hard and lay there, too dizzy to even attempt to rise. Waves of nausea swept over her and she clutched at her stomach, trying not to heave. She moaned, realizing that Aunt Hilda's anxious face was now looking down at her. Her aunt was speaking to her, calling for help, looking anything but comforting.

Doc Valentine came running down the hall, having just arrived at the hospital. Coattails flying, Auntie Belle right behind him, he had heard Aunt Hilda's frantic yell for help. He had never heard her sound that way before; frightened out of her wits, or scared to death. He had heard her usual tart reply or sharp retort, was used to that, though she usually saved it for others and not him. But he had never heard fear in her voice before. "What is it? Oh...here...let me see her. Did she hit her head? What happened?" he questioned, as he knelt beside Ophelia, checking her eyes, her pulse, surprised by her lack of response. He could tell she was disoriented, and his thoughts raced; going over page after page of medical information in his mind. Ophelia was always so strong, never one to faint or become ill. He glanced up as he heard the front door slam and saw Cal running down the hall toward them.

"Belle came and got me. What's happened...Ophelia..." Cal said as he knelt quickly beside his wife, looking anxiously at Doc.

"We need to get her into bed," Doc said, getting to his feet. Cal stood, lifting Ophelia up into his arms. He saw the way her eyes looked: glazed and frightened, and could feel how limp she was.

"It'll be all right, honey," he said, his heart beating rapidly as he made his way up the stairs to their rooms, and laid her gently down upon their bed. "I'm right here, Ophelia. You're going to be all right."

Ophelia groaned, not answering, then rolled onto her side and was sick. Cal jumped back, surprised, trying to avoid her vomit. "I'm sorry," Ophelia whispered, clenching her teeth and pushing one hand into her stomach. Aunt Hilda had just entered the room as Ophelia lost her breakfast on the floor beside the bed, and she quickly turned and headed back downstairs to get a basin of water and cloths to clean up both her niece and the floor, a worried frown upon her face.

Doc had raced up the stairs behind Ophelia's aunt, having gone to get his bag, his face red from hurrying. He waited while Ophelia and the floor were wiped up, then began his examination, asking Cal to go into the other room.

Cal did as he was asked, taking off his coat and throwing it down upon a straight-backed chair in the far corner, then settling down in a more comfortable chair nearest the door to the bedroom. He had never known Ophelia to be sick and wondered if she had become so because of the day she had run from him. He saw in his mind's eye how cold she had been when he caught up with her. Saw the bluish tinge to her skin and how she had shivered violently in his arms. He remembered how he had tried to warm her feet, rubbing them within his hands, and how she had sat there, not responding. It was all his fault, of that he was sure, and he felt anger fester inside him at how foolish he'd been. How unthinking of me, he thought. If only she hadn't heard. He bent forward, resting his head in his hands, wishing so much that he could take back that day. Wishing he could take back his words, and wishing—for that moment—that he had never met Lea. Lea, Lea, Lea, it had *always* been Lea, right from the first time he'd seen her. He'd been so taken with her. Hadn't been able to help himself. And *now*...now his foolishness had caused Ophelia not only undue pain and upset, but to become ill. He groaned softly, shaking his head, filled with overwhelming regret.

The memory came then of how he'd come to his senses, how he'd raced down the hall later, grabbing Ophelia, shouting his love for her, embarrassing her, and not caring. She'd been so surprised, and so pleased. He'd thought she was pleased, thought she had forgiven him and gotten over the sadness he'd caused by his foolish words. She'd laughed at him and returned his kisses, quieted him and stopped what she was doing—tending a patient who watched them with feverish brow and wide smile—and she'd gone back upstairs with him, letting him kiss her while he undressed her, letting him make love to her. He lifted his head, hearing faint sounds from their bedroom, wondering what was taking Doc so long. Memories flooded back; she had cried after they finished. Not in pain, but...as he thought of it now. ...not happy tears. And she had not been herself after that. No smiles greeted him in the mornings that followed. No cheery conversation, telling him to have a good day as he hurried out the door, heading to work at the Mercantile. No, it had been different after that. Ophelia had been different: quieter, not full of enthusiasm, not...herself. He blamed himself, wishing so much that he could take back his words that day, could start anew, could...what? And then he heard Doc call his name, and he stood, walking into the room where his wife lay, pale and weak, knowing that it was *he* who was to blame.

"I don't know what to tell you," Doc said, lowering his voice as he stood next to Cal at the foot of the bed. "It's too soon to tell just what made her faint. I'll keep checking on her today, make sure she's comfortable, and we'll see how things go, Cal. That's about all I can do for now. I've given her something to help her sleep. Imagine all the tending she's done of others, ever since the hospital opened, has caught up with her, exhausted her. That might be it." He glanced back at Ophelia, shaking his head. "A good woman, Cal. Always concerned for *others* and not taking much time for herself. I hold myself accountable, somewhat. I get so wrapped up in doctoring...never think about how much work others do. Ophelia's always been so reliable."

Cal nodded, looking down at the floor, wishing there was some word of hope that doc would offer. "She will get better, won't she?" he said, at last, a feeling of guilt washing over him. "*I'm* to blame, Doc, for not appreciating all she does, not only for the patients, but for *me*."

He looked away, not trusting himself to say more, feeling how choked up his voice had become.

"Now, now. Don't blame yourself, Cal. You have a job to do. The Mercantile can't run itself, you know. It's most likely she's just worn out. A little rest and she should be fine. Why, I'll bet in a week or so she'll be right back to working *twice as hard* to make up for the time she's off her feet."

"Thanks, Doc. Let me know, please, if there's any change, or if I'm needed, okay?" Cal said, noticing how pale his wife's face was.

"Will do, Cal. Will do," Doc said, and he turned and went down the stairs, seeing Aunt Hilda standing at the foot of the stairs, waiting for word of her niece.

Cal walked over to the side of the bed, bending to place a soft kiss upon Ophelia's forehead, noticing how warm she felt. She stirred, but didn't wake, and sadness filled Cal as he stood there. He'd make it up to her, he promised himself. He'd see to it, somehow, that she was happy again, no matter what it took. Hearing movement on the stairs, he looked up in time to see Aunt Hilda entering the room. "I'll sit with her a spell, if you don't mind," she said, and he nodded, mumbling something about relieving Auntie Belle, who had come to get him and was now watching the store. Then he turned and walked down the stairs, feeling a weight on him as heavy as *any* he had ever felt before.

CHAPTER 14

Michael was hard at work fixing fences when Colin rode into his place a few days later. He stopped working, wiping his brow, waiting while his brother dismounted and walked toward him. "What brings you out here, brother," he asked, noticing the heavy bedroll and bulging saddlebags on Colin's horse. "Going somewhere?"

Colin smiled, shaking his head in answer. "Feel the mountains calling me. Decided it was time to head on out and see the country," he said, looking across the field. "It's about time you got things fixed up around here."

Michael grinned at him. "You mean since my outlaw days are over?"

Colin gave him a stern look before answering. "They'd *better* be *over*, now that you got yourself a wife and all."

Michael shook his head. "Ain't that the truth. Lydia would skin me alive if I got a hankering to ride again." He stomped his foot so the snow fell off. "Let's go up to the house. She'll have a pot of coffee on the stove. You ate yet?"

"I had a bite before I did chores. Might be able to get some more down," Colin replied, walking beside his brother toward the house. They matched each other's stride.

"So, what do you mean, the mountains are calling you? Where you off to?" Michael asked, opening the door and going inside, Colin behind him.

"No need to stick around, the way I see it. Now that Maw's gone James can look after the farm. He'll marry himself a nice gal and settle in, one of these days, I'm sure," Colin said.

Yeah, the way that Yeager gal was tending him at Maw's lay- ing- out, I figure it won't be long and they'll be getting hitched, don't you think?" Michael asked, not seeing the look on Colin's face as he glanced down at the floor, more sure than ever that it was high time he moved on.

"Well, hello Colin," Lydia said, entering the kitchen from the side bedroom. "I wondered who was here. How are you?"

"Doing good," he said, noticing how nice she looked; her hair curled on top of her head, a large apron covering the front of the pale green dress she wore. Colin had to admit she looked like a different person, like a lady, even, not like the gal she used to be. He smiled, thinking how lucky it was that she and Michael had gotten together. It was obvious they were happy. Even more obvious that they loved each other, and Colin was glad. Maybe love was all it took to get a person to change their ways. Whatever it took, she sure looked pretty, smiling over at his brother like she was, and filled out some. When he'd first seen her at that little cabin over by Chaska, she'd been pencil-thin. It was a miracle the wind hadn't blown her away, he thought, and then he realized Michael was holding out a cup of coffee for him and he took it, his mood lifting somewhat.

"So, what's brought on this sudden urge to travel, brother?" Michael asked pulling out a chair and nodding toward another one.

"It's time, that's all," Colin answered, settling onto the chair.

"You and James have words?"

"Why would you think that?" Colin asked, frowning.

"Well, he gets that pretty gal fussing around him like a turkey ready to be plucked and stewed, and here you are, ready to move on. I just thought maybe there was a problem, that's all."

Colin snorted in reply, shaking his head, and took a long drink of his coffee. "Mighty good coffee, Lydia," he said, and he smiled at her as she stirred a large pot on the stove.

"Why, thank you, sir," she said, smiling back at him.

Michael watched him, still wondering why he had suddenly decided to leave. "Didn't Patrick say you had your eye on that Yeager gal, brother?"

Colin glanced at his brother, keeping his expression unreadable and shifted slightly before answering, "You know Patrick. He's always been one to know things there ain't no way to know. No, I think she's a pretty woman. Any man with eyes has to see that. But, no, we never courted, if that's what you're getting at." He felt Michael's gaze on him and wished he'd talk about something else.

"Are you glad to be back to Hastings, Lydia?" he asked, deciding *he'd* better change the subject. "Sure am," she said. "It's good to be back."

"I ran into Doc the other day at the Mercantile. He said your sister hasn't been feeling too good. Don't know what the problem is, but he said he's been doctoring her awhile."

Lydia bit her lip before answering, a sadness filling her eyes. "I guess maybe *I'm* the problem," she said, her voice a mere whisper.

"Why is that?" Colin asked, surprised that she'd think that.

"It's because of our boy," Michael cut in, his voice stern. "Eli. They, or rather *Lilly*, apparently didn't expect Lydia to ever come back to Hastings. And now that she has, it's ruffled Lilly's feathers."

"Now, Michael, you know she's been sick a long time. Even before I came back. She fell, that's when she first started feeling bad, Eli said. He says it hurts her to walk and bend. I...I went out to their place right after we came back, tried to talk to her, tell her how proud I was of the way she'd raised our boy." She hesitated, rubbing her arm with one hand and taking in a deep breath before continuing. "I never got the chance to tell her. She wasn't happy to see me."

"Well, I think you need to try again," Michael said. "I think we should just go on out there and have a talk with them. Jonas is a really nice fellow. Reasonable. He'll listen. We need to tell them how we feel. It ain't like we want to take Eli away from them. He's a grown man now. He told them right off that he wanted to get to know us, and wanted to spend time with us, too. They...er...well, Jonas seemed all right with that. Seems foolish, two sisters living this close, and not able to act like sisters should. Look at those old gals at the hospital, the aunts. That cranky one bosses the smiley one around all the time, but they're still close."

Both Colin and Lydia laughed aloud at this. "They sure are a pair, aren't they?" Colin said, a wide smile upon his face.

"Well, there's a big change coming, I heard," Lydia said. "I was in the Mercantile the other day, and Auntie Belle told me she's getting married. Isn't that the nicest thing you ever heard?"

"Who to?" Michael and Colin asked at the same time.

"To Juliana's grandfather, Jacob Wright," Lydia answered. "I thought you knew, Colin."

"How would I know?"

"Well, Auntie Belle said he asked her the day of your maw's laying-out. Seems Belle had gone outside, thinking he was angry with her, and not knowing why it might be, she'd decided to go on back to the hospital. She ran out and got into the buggy, and here he comes and climbs right in beside her, and asks her to be his wife! I just think that's the most romantic thing I've ever heard."

Colin laughed aloud, setting his empty cup on the table. "Well, that's sure a happier thing to do than what we were doing." It was Michael's turn to snort in reply.

"I didn't think it was very proper," Michael said. "But, he needs someone to tend his grandchildren, I suppose. And Auntie Belle sure is a fine lady. Don't think he could have found a better one."

"You got that right," Colin answered, looking into the fire, his thoughts rushing back to his own wedding day, the summer of 1859. Gabby coming toward him down the isle in the church, her lovely face radiant. A vision of loveliness, she beamed with joy. Resplendent in a gown of shimmering white, her dark tresses piled high upon her head, she looked like an angel, he remembered thinking. *His* angel, her joy as boundless as his own. *His* angel, so very happy and so very lovely.

"*Colin*," Michael's voice burst into his reveries like the crack of a rifle, shattering the images in his head.

"What?" he asked, looking over at his brother, seeing the look on his face. A questioning look.

"Are you all right? I asked if you wanted some stew, but you were miles away. What's bothering you?" Michael asked, reaching out to take the bowl of steaming stew Lydia handed him. He placed it in front of Colin, a concerned look upon his face.

"I'm fine," Colin replied, shifting in his chair, picking up a slice of homemade bread and dunking it into the stew. "I was just thinking. I'm trying to decide which way to head on out, that's all."

"So which way are you going?"

Colin finished the bite of stew, shaking his head, before answering. "Dog-goned if I know. Thought I'd just head west, maybe go see Mary. Sent her a letter about Maw passing, and I thought she might like a little company from home."

"Good idea," Michael said, cutting off a slice of bread and buttering it. "A lot has changed since she went off with that Dawson fellow. I've been thinking about her a lot, myself, since Maw...you know. Been wondering how she's doing, if she's happy. Dawson seemed like a good fellow, though I never did understand his wife killing herself...something real strange about that."

"Well, folks don't always know what drives a person to make the choices they do, even if they know that person well," Colin said, and he got up, taking his bowl over to the stove so Lydia could scoop him up a second bowl of the delicious stew. "Thanks," he said, and he resumed his seat. "I heard about that, but don't know why she'd do such a thing. I guess that's something only the good Lord understands. Some folks put on a brave front, smiling a lot, when inside they've got something eating on them that they can't shake. It isn't like in a war, that's understandable...the pain and suffering and all. People expect grief and suffering...and the dying that comes with war. It just doesn't seem to make much sense; a woman...a mother with a whole passel of young'uns, ending it like she did. Strange, indeed. I hope Mary's happy with Dawson. He seemed like a good fellow, or so Maw said. She said he was a hard worker; worked at that store of his from sunup to sunset, every day but on the Sabbath. That's got to say something for him. He wasn't a drinker or anything like that, from what I heard." He took another bite of stew before continuing.

"And Mary wouldn't have gone off with someone who was. Of course I didn't really get to know her all that much, being away so long. Maw said she had gotten attached to the Dawson young'uns while she tended them when their maw first took sick. She said, young as Mary was, she knew her mind. She wanted to be their mother and there was no shaking her from it." He scraped his bowl clean and leaned back in his chair, stretching. "I guess I'll just head that way and see for myself, and see the country while I'm at it."

"Sounds like a plan," Michael stated, setting his bowl aside, too, and smiling over at Lydia as she lifted a large pan of water onto the stove. "I'd go with you, brother, if this woman here didn't have a firm hold on me." He laughed, seeing the frown on Lydia's face, and how her eyebrows raised at hearing these words. "But she just won't let me go. Never met such a good man as me, she says." Lydia blushed at his teasing, and Colin hoped his face showed no trace of the color he felt spreading across it.

"Looks like you better stay right here, Michael, and count your blessings. A man who has a good woman's love, doesn't need to ride off to see the country," Colin said, and both Michael and Lydia could not help noticing the sad look in his eyes as he spoke, and wondered if Colin was speaking from experience.

"I hope you find that kind of love, too, brother," Michael said, and he reached over, gently squeezing Colin's shoulder.

Colin smiled, then gave Lydia a quick hug, and with firm grip, shook his brother's hand. It was time to leave, no more looking back.

CHAPTER 15

Father Patrick rose from his knees, his thoughts far from the prayers he'd just prayed. He sat back upon the bench closest the altar, gazing at his surroundings as though seeing them for the first time: the large crucifix hanging behind the altar, the poignant figure of the Lord nailed there, blood visible at the sight of each wound, the crown of thorns piercing His forehead. To one side a wooden tray of lit candles, the flames flickering, the statue of Jesus' mother nearby. He bowed his head, placing a hand on either side, and took in a deep breath. So much had changed in the weeks just passed. Unexpected changes; first, his maw's death, and now Colin leaving. He'd never expected that. It was a good thing, he supposed. Colin had never been one to stay put very long. His thoughts turned back to the first time he remembered him leaving. He'd been young then, not yet a man. Colin had suddenly decided to go, and though it brought great sadness to their maw, she had said nothing, he remembered. She knew, of all her sons, that it would do no good. Colin had always been the one with a hankering for far distant places. She had even laughed about it, once, telling their paw that Colin had an adventuresome streak as wide as their pasture. When he did decide to go, however, it hadn't made her laugh. Patrick had heard her crying at night, when all else was still in their house. Even his paw hadn't been able to comfort her, though he had tried. Patrick took in a deep breath, memories assailing him.

Colin seemed driven to leave, driven to venture forth, seeking adventure—or whatever it was—that stirred this restlessness inside him. It was as if he was searching for something, an elusive some-thing, just beyond his grasp. It would be no different this time, Patrick thought. It was just the way his brother was. He thought about how hard it had been on their folks after Colin had left: the hard work needing to be done around the place, and only him and Michael to help. William was away then, working at a distant ranch, and James had either been sick abed, or off teaching at the little settlement to the East. With their paw not in good health, his breathing labored and always having had such terrible spells and having to go to bed for days, there'd been just the two boys and their maw to tend the animals and get the planting done. Michael resented having to do so much work, and left shortly after, when Sheriff Gentry offered him a wage for doing the same work. And I, Patrick thought, I was small, *too small* to do it all alone. He shook his head. I did my best, working side-by-side with Maw. Even when I broke my arm, and later my leg, I tried to keep everything up. He rubbed a hand across his forehead, remembering how difficult it had been; the blisters on his hands from plowing each spring, the painful thumb he'd had when he tried to fix the fence one winter, his hands so cold that the hammer had slipped and smashed his thumb, and how he'd tried not to cry because it hurt so badly, and had felt the tears freeze upon his cheeks.

He shook his head, saddened by all these memories. He never resented Colin's leaving, like Michael had. He'd just done the best he could, done what Maw asked of him. It pleased him when he saw the relief she felt, knowing the chores were done; stalls cleaned, the cow fed, fences mended. He felt proud of himself, felt like he'd made up for the...*other* things. The things that—try as he might—he couldn't explain to her. Later he'd told her; explaining about the things he'd seen, and why he'd done what he'd done. He told her about the lady in the silvery-white gown and light blue robe, her eyes filled with love, her hands reaching out to him, her voice musical, like a whisper on the wind. He told her what the lady had said to him, how she told him things that touched his heart, though never once had he seen her lips move when she spoke. She'd told him he had a special gift, that not everybody could see her like he could, or hear her. She told him if he listened—*really listened*—not like others listen, but with his *heart,* she would guide and protect him always. All he had to do in return was to take her Son's message to those who needed it, then she would guide him where best he could serve.

Patrick sat up straight, a slight smile upon his face as he thought these things. "I never doubted you, even once," he said, his voice a mere whisper in the stillness of the church. "I have *always* believed in your Son and followed His leading, *never once* doubting" he said, his eyes filling with tears. "You led me through the swarm of angry Pawnee to save Jacob Wright's grandchildren, guiding my footsteps. You've kept me safe through so many, many perils, ever since I was young, Blessed Mother. Why do I feel such loss now...not only at Maw's passing, but at Colin's leaving? I feel a great emptiness. A sorrow so great inside of me that I weep with shame at telling you. The people come flocking to the church, their smiling faces showing their pleasure at having this grand church to worship in, and to sustain them through their joys and sorrows. They come willingly, bringing their children, teaching them. They bring their troubles and lay them at your dear Son's feet, seeking His guidance and wisdom. They bring their joy, celebrating the sacraments, opening their hearts to God's wondrous love."

He closed his eyes, feeling contentment flood through him. "Dearest Lord, guide me where You want me to go. I, *too,* feel a restlessness within me. Like my brother, I wish to journey from here. You know of the great suffering farther west, between the settlers and the Indians. If only I might serve You there. If only I could bring God's Word to both the whites *and* Indian people." Patrick opened his eyes, surprise showing in them. Until that moment, he hadn't realized he wanted to leave. He hadn't realized his restlessness was due to the feeling that it was time for him to move on. He stood, walking toward the altar, then knelt and bowed his head. In the stillness of the church, the flames from the many small candles flickered, casting dancing shadows against the walls and lighting the painted eyes of the statues of saints residing there. Silence filled the church as Father Patrick finished praying, made the sign of the cross, and got to his feet. It did not surprise him that silence was his only companion. Nor did it surprise him that the Lady had not appeared. It was enough that he had prayed. He knew, *without doubt*, that in God's *own time* his prayers would be answered. It was *always* that way. "Ask and ye shall receive," that's what the Bible said, and he believed it with *all his heart*. Patrick O'Leary *knew* an answer would come, when *God* was ready. "Thank you," he whispered, "and please watch over my brother, Colin, wherever the road may lead him. Amen," he added, turning to go finish the paperwork he had begun much earlier that morning.

CHAPTER 16

Jonas Hart lay his paperwork aside as he noticed a buggy coming up the lane toward his house. He called to Lilly that they had company, and was surprised when he saw that it was Michael and Lydia who stepped down from the buggy. He wondered how that would affect his wife, who had not spoken to her sister since she'd come back to Hastings. He wondered, too, where Eli was, and if he should call him. Instead, he walked slowly to the door, opening it just as Michael and Lydia stepped up to it.

"Well, hello," he said, smiling at them. "Come on in." He stepped back, ushering them into the warmth of the front parlor where he enjoyed sitting, looking over his papers and soaking up the warmth from the fireplace there. "Let me take your coats," he offered, reaching out to help Lydia off with hers. "Be seated. I'll tell Lilly you're here." He walked out to the kitchen to find his wife sitting at the kitchen table, staring at him with an anxious look upon her face. He walked to her, smiling tenderly at the woman he had loved ever since he was a young man. "Come on, Lilly. It'll be all right. Let's see what they want. I'm sure it'll be all right. I'll be right beside you. Please, sweetheart..."

Lilly looked at him, wondering how he could be so calm. *She* certainly didn't feel it. She took a deep breath, not moving, and not answering. She saw the streaks of gray in her husband's hair, the caring look in his eyes, the tender smile upon his lips. Always he was like this. No matter what happened, he was her rock, her strong yet gentle husband, never wavering in his love for her. She brushed back a strand of hair, not smiling, but rising. Placing her hand in his, she stood, slightly unsteady at first. "All right. I suppose we have to see them. Let's get it over with. Jonas smiled once more at her, and looked over at the stove. Lilly followed his gaze, understanding without words being spoken, what he was thinking. "I'll make a fresh pot of coffee," she said. Jonas was pleased by this and squeezed her hand, then turned and walked back into the front parlor, telling their unexpected guests that Lilly would be right in, she was making coffee.

Lydia cleared her throat, asking in a mere whisper, "Would it be all right if I go see if she needs any help?"

Jonas and Michael exchanged matching looks of concern, then Jonas said he thought that was a fine idea. Lydia stood, walking toward the kitchen, her heart pounding inside her like a drum. She couldn't help remembering the last time she'd come to the farm and what a terrible mistake it had been. She hoped with all her heart that it would not end up the same, today. She paused as she entered the room, seeing how pale Lilly looked, how sad she looked, and how she had aged. It surprised her, but she had heard that her sister had been ill, and it was evident. "Lilly," she said, and she took a deep breath, not knowing what to expect.

"Hello, Lydia."

"Hello. It's nice of you to...to..." Lydia wasn't good at small talk, and stopped talking without finishing whatever it was she had intended to say. She fidgeted, still standing where she was.

"You might as well sit down," Lilly said, her voice sounding as tired as she looked. Lydia noticed that her sister did not look at her, and even avoided looking in her direction as she spoke.

"Maybe I should just go back in the...other room," Lydia said.

"Do as you please," Lilly answered, still not looking her way.

Lydia hesitated, turning back toward the parlor, then stopped and again turned toward her sister. She walked into the kitchen, pulled out a chair and sat down. "It was Michael's idea to come today," she said, forcing herself to speak. "He knows how bad I've felt about...my last visit." Lilly stood, her back to Lydia, hearing her words, but not turning, or even moving. "I...miss you, Lilly. I've missed you for a long, long time." Lydia took in a deep breath before continuing. "I know I've made a lot of mistakes. A lot of *horrible* mistakes that have hurt...*everybody*...especially you, sister. I'm so sorry. I wish you could find it in your heart...to forgive me...please." Lydia's voice broke and she began to cry. She quickly reached into her pocket for a handkerchief, and finding one, muffled the sound of her crying. When she could regain her composure she looked up, surprised to see that Lilly had moved and now sat across the table from her. She sniffled, wiping away her tears. The silence hung between them like a shroud.

After a few moments, Lilly spoke, her voice sounding lifeless, and filled with despair. "And you think your words will soften my heart? A few tears and all is *forgiven*, sister?" She emphasized the word, and sat up straighter, a challenging look upon her face. "What is it you want from me? Is it my *forgiveness* for your shameful actions? Or is it really my *son* you want?" Lilly glared at Lydia, all the shame and painful embarrassment she had felt over the years adding fire to the anger that burned inside her. "He will not be 'bought' with your tears, Lydia. Not after all the tears you have caused with your shameful living." Her words cut into Lydia, who hung her head and willed herself to endure the cruelty of them. She realized only now how badly she had hurt Lilly, and forced herself to sit quietly, not arguing or giving the slightest response. There was *nothing* she could say that would do any good, she realized. Slowly she raised her head and straightened in the chair so that her gaze met her sister's. Then, after a few moments of silence, she stood and walked slowly from the room and back into the parlor, without a word.

The two men stood as she walked toward them, aware that Lydia had been crying. "What is it?" Michael asked, reaching over to take her hand. Jonas sat still, wondering what to do. Should he go to Lilly, or stay where he was, waiting to hear what had happened?

"It's no use," Lydia said, smiling sadly in Jonas' direction. "I asked her forgiveness, and she *can't* forgive me." Her eyes once more teared up, and she dabbed at them with her handerchief, sniffling.

"This is *foolishness*," Michael stated, rising. "I'll talk to her."

Jonas rose, blocking the younger man's way. "You'll do *no such thing,*" he stated, adamantly. "This is *my* house, and if my wife feels as she does, *you'll* not..." his voice had risen angrily, much to everyone's surprise, his large hands drawing up into fists.

"Pa! What's going on?" Eli exclaimed, as he bounded down the stairs from his room, having heard the angry words. "Michael. I didn't know you were here. What's the matter?"

"I'll tell you what's the matter," Michael roared, his face red and hands clenched. "Lydia came to apologize, and your...Lilly...*ain't decent enough* to forgive her."

Jonas lashed out, his large fist slamming into Michael's jaw, knocking him down. "You'll *not* be talking about my wife like that!" Jonas yelled, as Lilly rushed into the room.

"Stop! *Stop this instant!*" she screamed, as Michael lurched to his feet, his hands drawn up, ready to fight. Lydia, too, was screaming at the men and trying to pull Michael back and stop the brawl.

To everyone's amazement, Eli rushed to stand between the two men, his face redder than both of theirs, his eyes flashing with anger. He looked at Jonas first, then turned and glared at Michael, his hands also drawn up in fists. "So *this* is how it is!" he shouted. "This is what it's come to!" He glanced over at Lydia, then back at Lilly, fierce anger blazing in his eyes. He shook his head, noticing Jonas lower his hands, biting his lip, no longer a look of anger upon his face. Michael stood glaring, however, his fists at the ready.

"If you keep your fists up, Michael, it's *me* you'll have to fight. Do you want that? Will *that* mend the way you feel?" Eli asked, standing his ground.

"I'll not be knocked down by the likes of him," Michael said, swearing aloud, even though the women were in the room.

"Then we'll step outside," Eli said, his tone matching his father's. "Let's go!"

"No!" both women cried, afraid for their son.

"You'll *not* be going anywhere," Jonas said, laying his hand on Eli's shoulder. "This isn't your fight, son."

Eli turned on him, asking, "Then who's fight is it? *Yours?* You've done *nothing* to cause it. You've raised me right, taught me all the things I know, showed me nothing but *kindness and love* all my life. Is it *your* fight, then?" Eli questioned, and then he turned back to Michael. "You didn't know I was your son when I was born. But you became my friend over the years. My *best* friend! A friend who taught me to dance, and explained about..." he hesitated slightly "...about girls. A friend who cared about me even *before* you knew I was your son. Is it *your* fight, then?" Michael's fists lowered as Eli spoke, and he felt shamed by Eli's words.

Then Eli turned to face the women, though he continued to stand where he was, separating the two men. "And you," he said, his voice softening only slightly as he looked at Lilly. "Are you happy to go around the house all day, grieving and feeling bad because you're so afraid of losing me? And you," he said, looking at Lydia, "do you think a few words can heal your sister's heart?" Saying this, he reached to the sheath at his side, pulling out his knife, holding it blade up as he turned slowly in a circle, all four of his parents backing up, shocked by his actions. "*This* is what it's come to then," Eli stated raising his other hand, palm up, exposing his wrist, his gaze going from one to the other of his terrified mothers and then to both men he loved as his father. "Is it a *piece of me* you want?" he asked. "*One* for you and Lydia, Michael, and *one* for you and Lilly, Jonas? Isn't that the way such a problem was solved in the Bible? The baby must be *cut in half* am I right? Well, here I am, and if that's what it takes..." his words ended as he made a swipe with the knife! Both women screamed, and Jonas and Michael lunged forward, each seizing one of Eli's arms *before* the deed could be done!

"What the hell, son," Michael said, his face pale, as he clutched Eli's arm.

"Dear Lord, son," Jonas said at the same time, not loosening his hold on Eli's other arm.

Both women rushed forward, wrapping their arms about Eli, their sobs filling the room, relief showing upon their faces. Eli stood silent, looking from one to the other, a slight smile upon his face. Any other man might have been taking a chance, doing what he'd done. But he knew his parent*s*—*all of them*—loved him, and he trusted, *beyond a doubt,* that they would *not* let his knife do its terrible work.

When the women stopped crying and pulled away from him, and Jonas and Michael finally let go of his arms, Eli spoke, "I'm *not* a prize for the taking. Not one of you can *own* me. But I love you—*all of you*—and know you all love me. It's time to forgive and forget the past. If I can, you should all be able to, too. How about it?"

In a few moments, Michael and Jonas were shaking hands and laughing together, neither mentioning the angry red mark on Michael's cheek where Jonas had hit him. And Lilly and Lydia were hugging and both talking and crying, at once, while Eli slid his knife back into its sheath, a satisfied look upon his face. And in the kitchen, the coffee became too strong to drink, as it continued to boil upon the stove.

CHAPTER 17

Those who lived in Hastings, that December, all agreed that the most joyous celebration that year had been the marrying of Miss Dorothea Blossom to Jacob Wright. The little church on Old Mill Road was filled far beyond capacity—even quite a few of the town's Catholics attending—as Jacob Wright placed a ring on Auntie Belle's finger. He'd carved the ring, sitting up late into the night to do so, the week before the wedding. It was made of pine and notched all around to resemble a circle of blossoms—much to Belle's delight—and he'd rubbed it until it shined. He'd been quick to promise to replace it with a "real" ring of silver or gold, first chance he got. But Belle had cried with happiness when she saw it, and vowed to never take it off, telling him *no other* could *ever* mean as much. The Wright children had sat wide-eyed in the front row of the little church, sharing a few pokes and pushes until Jacob cleared his throat to settle them, and after that they smiled angelically.

Belle looked beautiful in a new dress that her sister had helped her make, and the smile upon her lovely face gave credence to the joy she felt. Her eyes twinkled above the rosy blush of her cheeks, and her soft white hair fluffed around her head like gossamer. And never once did she cry, though there was plenty of that going on! Aunt Hilda led the crying, covering her mouth with her handkerchief, and there wasn't a dry eye in the house amongst the other women there. Tears of joy flowed like wine, and a cheer from the men could be heard all the way to Jonas Hart's farm when Jacob bent to kiss his bride. Auntie Belle smiled and blushed, squeezing his hand within hers. And everyone laughed when she halted as they walked down the aisle, and bent to place a quick kiss on Father Patrick's cheek. After that, *his* face was redder than hers. It would be hard to say who meant more to the townsfolk; Auntie Belle with her gentle, sweet-natured, caring ways, or Jacob with his forthright manner and kindly disposition. It was a marriage between two fine people, and it brought a joyous satisfaction to all who knew them.

A week later, Christmas filled hearts with joy, as mothers brought out gifts of mittens and dolls and such, that they had made for their little ones, and fathers trudged off into the woods, coming back with trees in tow to be decorated with strips of cloth and paper and cranberries strung on string. And cookies or other simple treats often graced a plate upon the table. Almost every one of the townsfolk—the adults, that is— attended church that year, singing their hearts out and thanking the Lord for their blessings. Why even some of the girls from the houses down by the docks arrived in time for Mass, Father Patrick noticed, trying *not* to notice how some winked at him and giggled, wiggling their fingers in greeting. He shook his head, praying that his cheeks would not still be flaming when he took his place at the altar. And in the little church on Old Mill Road—long after the singing had already begun—the doors flew open letting in a sudden gust of cold air that chilled everyone, when Sheriff "Gator" MacKay strode in smelling strongly of cigarette smoke and the Lucky Lady Saloon.

Yes, it was a time of celebration, everyone in town would agree. Except, that is, for Cal Dunnevey and the aunts: Annathea Blossom and Dorothea Wright. They could not share in the Christmas spirit, though Auntie Belle and Jacob *did* attend church on Christmas morning. They smiled in return when greeted, but it was sadness and worry that shone in their eyes. Like most of the other children in town, his grandchildren remained at home as Doc had suggested. Doc and his wife, Judith, and Aunt Hilda did *not* attend, keeping instead their tireless vigil at the hospital. The hospital had only six patients: five children covered with spots and suffering raging fevers, and Cal's wife, Ophelia Dunnevey; the fine lady who had opened her lovely home as a hospital. And in spite of the many prayers that were said that Christmas morning in both churches for Miz Dunnevey and those youngsters, it was a Christmas that few would not soon forget.

Three days after Ophelia fainted in the hallway of the hospital, a feverish attack occurred. Two days later, as with the five children, a bright scarlet rash appeared all over her body and within her mouth and about the fauces—the cavity at the back of her mouth. Upon seeing this, Doc knew he had been correct in his suspicion that Scarlet Fever had come to Hastings.

Immediately he put out the word that there was chance of an epidemic in town, and that it was best that all the young children, in particular, not leave their homes. Scarlet Fever could attack with a vengence, or in a milder form that—in some cases—would *not* require medicine, simply rest. It was not unusual for *both* types to be prevalent at one time, as was the case with those in his care. Three of the children had a milder form, and two others and Miz Dunnevey suffered the more serious type. Both were highly contagious. In the milder form, the rash had first appeared around the children's necks, spreading the very next day to cover their whole bodies. The fourth day, which was on Christmas, the eruption was at its worst; the mouth and fauces red and sore, with little red points appearing on the tongue and rising up through the white crust that covered it. In two of the children this crust had already come off, leaving not only the complete area as red as a strawberry and terribly sore, but also their faces and throats swollen.

Judith and Aunt Hilda rushed from child to child, giving drinks of warm lemonade with gum Arabic dissolved in it, and saw to it they were covered with a piece of dry flannel. Sheets were then wrung out in boiling hot water and laid upon their stomachs, having to be removed as quickly as possible once they became cool. This remedy Doc had been given by an eminent physician from the East, who insisted he had cured 99 out of 100 cases. Doc hoped it would prove true for his patients as well. The wet sheets required repeated heating until perspiration broke out, at which time the children would be on the road to recovery. Judith and Aunt Hilda hurried from room to room tending their charges, a most tiring and difficult work, yet they struggled on, not giving in to fatigue.

Doc, alone, tended those stricken with the more severe form of the fever, wondering how many others might have been contaminated. He knew first signs didn't show until a week after contamination, and it was possible for whole schools of children to catch it. Wiping his brow, he raced among the three seriously ill children and then upstairs to tend Ophelia, praying a silent prayer that this would not become the case in Hastings. Night and day, he, Judith and Aunt Hilda were on their feet, catching only moments of sleep—little of it restful—and he wondered how long they could keep up the pace.

Ophelia—like the two sickest children—lay abed, her fever a raging 108 on the thermometer. Her voice was thick when she tried to speak and she complained of stiffness and pain on trying to move her neck. Doc checked her pulse often, as it was frequent but feeble. Large pieces of skin kept coming off, as was usual, especially from her hands and feet, but that was not what worried him most. Ophelia's throat was swollen and inflamed and slight ulcerations formed at the back of her mouth. White specks could be seen intermixed with the redness, and thick phlegm was constantly clogging her throat. He knew, without a doubt, that she and the three more seriously ill children were suffering from Malignant Scarlet Fever, also called Putrid Sore Throat. This form of the disease was particularly severe. If a patient did not die, they were often debilitated, suffering coughs and breathing trouble and fevers the rest of their lives. Strong beef tea was given in as large quantities as possible, along with wine, and the throat was injected with strong cleaning gargles. The infusion of cayenne pepper or a decoction of bark acidulated with sulphuric or muriatic acid, or gargles to which a little tincture of myrrh or camphor was added was the only treatments he knew, and he did what he could, having the ingredients needed, on hand. However—though he didn't tell Aunt Hilda straight out—only Cal, he also knew that *all* of these treatments were usually useless, and that there was no more fatal disease known.

Cal Dunnevey had never prayed so hard before as he did that Christmas morning and the days that followed. Doc had ordered him to not come to the hospital, telling him Ophelia would not know of his presence, anyway. He explained that as contagious as the fever was, it would not do for him to take a chance on spreading it. As it was, Doc and Judith were exhausted, as was Aunt Hilda, and Doc wondered how long they could carry on. They worked and ate and grabbed what little sleep they could, pushing themselves so others would not come to help and risk being exposed. Doc knew that extensive work lay ahead, too, in the burning of the patients' clothing, and the scrubbing of each and every surface, once the disease had finished reeking its destruction. It was imperative that they all carry on as they were, praying and trusting the Lord to see them through. He had told Cal, the very first day when Ophelia fainted, to pray as he never had before, knowing his prayers would help more than anything.

Days later, only the *least* sick of the children had survived, and fourteen new cases were being tended. Ophelia Denton Dunnevey and the other two children, however, had passed beyond their earthly cares.

CHAPTER 18

The new year began with more grief and sadness than was ever seen at one time in Hastings. Graves were dug in alarming numbers in both the cemetery in town and on homesteads. Smiles were rarely seen when one shopped or rode through town, black the predominant color of clothing. When the scourge was finished, the number of dead stood at seventeen; sixteen children ranging in age from fourteen months to fifteen years, and one adult: Ophelia Dunnevey.

Cal Dunnevey was devastated by the loss of his wife, managing to get through her funeral and burial by force of willpower alone. He could not sleep, nor eat, and avoided any and all signs of condolence given him. He also avoided both of Ophelia's aunts, certain that they blamed *him* for Ophelia's death. Truth was, he blamed himself, and no one could convince him different. Doc had tried to talk to him, tried in vain to explain that it was the fever that had caused her death. But Cal only stared at him, saying nothing, his eyes filled with remorse. Unable to stay in their rooms at the hospital, he had moved back into the small room at the back of the Mercantile and laid awake most nights, staring at the ceiling, his thoughts as black as the sky. Memories tore at him no matter where he was; and he thought he'd go mad. If only I could ride away, he thought, and never look back. If only I could distance myself from Hastings. Yet he felt powerless to do even the normal everyday things, let alone leave. He felt numbed by Ophelia's loss, and devastated by the overpowering shame and guilt that invaded his every waking hour. If only, he thought, again. Hour after hour, minute after minute, 'if only' became his mantra, imprisoning him as totally as ever an actual jail could.

Days that he could function he ran the store, waiting on his customers without giving his usual greeting or smile. Getting through the necessary progression of each day as if he, too, had died. He found himself unable to indulge in conversation and simply went through the motions of working and living. Some days he lay upon his cot in the backroom, not unlocking the door to customers, or caring. Those days he did not shave or wash, often laying abed in the same clothes he had worn countless numbers of days. He knew he should get up, should tend to his personal ablutions, should eat and shave and change his shirt and pants. He knew these things, but found himself incapable of doing so. Another man might have turned to drink to assuage feelings such as those that tormented him, but Cal had never found comfort in strong drink, and could not do so, even under such circumstances. He was adrift in a world of happy, smiling people, adrift on a sea of regret and remorse, and wondered if he might expire, his grief was so great.

On the second Sunday in January, after church, Jacob Wright made the short journey into town. Aunt Hilda was at the cabin visiting with Belle, and he decided that was a good time to drop in on Cal. It was a gloriously sunny day, and the sun warmed him as he rode along, his thoughts on what he would say to the younger man. After all, it had not been all that long ago that he had suffered the loss of his own wife, and he considered it his Christian duty to try to ease the suffering of Belle's nephew-by-marriage, if he could. If nothing else, it would give his dear Belle some peace of mind to know that he'd talked to Cal, he was sure.

He rode along, enjoying the peace and quiet, and was soon humming aloud. When he realized it, he grew quiet in surprise. It had been a long, long time since he'd remembered a tune, much less that *particular* tune. It had been his wife's favorite. He strained to think of its name, then gave up in disgust. Oh, well, he thought at last, at least my memory *is* returning, little by little.

He nodded to some folks in a buckboard that passed, again thinking of what he could say to Cal. He had been spared, for the time being, not being able to remember *his* wife's passing, his memory blocking the horror of it. He remembered the Pawnee riding toward them, remembered noticing the war paint upon their faces. After that, he remembered calling out his wife's name at the hospital in Hastings, and as he shouted it, a young girl had raced into the room, crying and hugging him, telling him she was his granddaughter, Juliana. "Juliana," he said aloud, wishing it would bring back more memories. "Juliana," he said again, then shouted it out as loud as he could, appealing to God in His mercy to help him remember.

He shook his head, sighing. He was married now to Belle. Married, and so very happy. Belle was a wonderful woman, always so kind to him and his grandchildren. A good cook and housekeeper. He could not have made a better choice of wife if he had tried. He smiled, remembering their wedding night. He had offered again to sleep in the boys' room, if she wished it. But Belle had taken his hand, leading him into their room, shutting the door behind him and—blushing furiously— had climbed into their bed, after asking him which side he preferred. He'd been almost as shy as she, not wanting to frighten or offend her, he remembered, and slid quickly beneath the blankets as soon as he dropped his drawers. A great silence followed, and both had lain as if suddenly turned to stone, barely breathing. When at last he could stand the silence no more, he had reached over and taken her hand, drawing it up to his lips, placing a gentle kiss upon it. To his surprise, Belle had giggled and rolled onto her side to face him. There was a smile upon her face that warmed his heart, and he felt as comfortable as if he had known her all his life. He raised up on one elbow, looking down at her. "Am I crowding you, Belle," he asked, watching her cheeks become a brighter shade of pink. She shook her head in answer, a shy smile upon her lips. "If there's anything you need...to make you happy here, dear lady, just let me know. If the children need speaking to, or if there's anything you'd like..." his words trailed off, as she reached up to touch his beard, her fingers stroking it gently. He said nothing, so pleased was he by such a tender gesture.

"There is something," Belle said, her voice a mere whisper.

"Name it, then," he answered, giving her his full attention.

"I...I'd like you to kiss me," Belle answered, timidly, and the kiss he gave her that night had been the first of many.

Jacob smiled, thinking how very fortunate he had been to find such a special woman. In only a matter of weeks he had come to feel great affection for her, and was certain she felt the same. He thought back to the day word had come that her niece, Ophelia, had died. Belle had rushed into his arms, wetting his shirt with her tears, and he'd held her and comforted her. He'd been surprised and pleased when she turned to him, and it made him feel all the closer to her. The children had watched, wide-eyed, as he stood there, his arms around her. Then Juliana drew near, patting Belle's shoulder to show her comfort. And when Belle walked over and sat in the rocking chair before the fireplace, her cheeks damp with tears, Mary had crawled up into her lap, snuggling her small face into the curve of Belle's neck. Jacob smiled, knowing it was in that moment that he'd realized that there was already a feeling of belonging being felt by his grandchildren, and it had pleased him immensely. As new as they all were to each other, they had already begun to be a family.

Pulling up in front of the Mercantile, he saw that the door was closed, and there was no sign of movement inside. He tied up at the hitching rail, then walked across the boardwalk to the double doors of the store, rapping on them. There was no answer. He rapped harder. Still no answer. Then he pounded, knowing he was drawing attention to himself, but not caring, having heard how deeply Cal was grieving.

In a few minutes, Cal opened the door, staring at him with eyes that squinted into the outside light. "What do you want?" he asked, not bothering to say hello. "I was sleeping. What time is it?"

"It's nearly two," Jacob replied, surprised to see the wrinkled shirt Cal wore, a stain running down the front. Unshaven, and his hair badly in need of brushing, it looked as if Cal hadn't slept in a month.

"Come in, if you want. What do you need?"

"Don't need anything," Jacob answered. "Just came to talk a spell. Aunt Hilda's out visiting with Belle and the children, and I thought it best I hightail it out of there and head to town. Thought maybe you might want a little company."

"No. I don't," Cal said. "But since you're already here, I guess it can't hurt." He attempted to smile, but though it showed upon his lips, the smile never reached his eyes. He looked haggard and worn, not to mention, beaten and bedeviled. He led the way back to his room at the back of the store, nodding toward a chair as he slumped onto his cot.

"You've got a nice store here," Jacob said.

Cal shrugged, not answering. Then he asked, "Want to buy it?"

Jacob looked at him, praying silently for some words that might reach the younger man. "What would you do, if you sold it?"

Cal laughed a hollow sounding laugh. "What difference does it make? Maybe I'd head on out...go somewhere. Get the hell out of here, that's for sure."

"I like Hastings," Jacob said. "I'm lucky I ended up here, though I still don't remember how I got here. The people have been downright kind to me and my grandchildren; seeing to it we've got a nice warm cabin to stay in and most of the necessities we need. It's not often that total strangers are treated so kindly, I imagine. I'll be glad when I can repay their kindness to us. If I had the money, I just might take you up on your question."

"What question is that?" Cal asked, not remembering.

"You asked me if I wanted to buy your store. I wouldn't mind it, if I had the money. I've been asking around town, looking for a job to tide us over until planting season comes. Now that Belle's my wife I don't want her to think I'm a slacker." He smiled, thinking of her, and was pleased to see Cal smile, too.

"She's something, isn't she?" Cal said. "I told Ophelia..." his words drifted off.

Jacob rose, changing the subject. "Do you mind if I put on a pot of coffee, Cal? I sure could use a cup."

Cal nodded toward the stove, saying nothing.

When the rich aroma of the hickory coffee filled the air, Jacob took down two cups, filling them, then resumed his seat. "I have a lot more memories now. Memories of the attack that day. I can see it so clear sometimes. There were eight Pawnee...or maybe ten...their dark hair sparse. Angry faces, painted faces, and some had painted their bodies. They wore buckskin pants and rode as if their horses were part of them." He stared down at the table, no longer talking for Cal's benefit, but because he was remembering. "I heard their cries, eerie cries that frightened the women. My wife...." he stopped abruptly, looking over at Cal, his heart pounding in his chest.

"Are you all right?" Cal asked, noticing how pale the older man's face had gotten. He stood, walking over to Jacob, resting his hand on his shoulder. "Are you all right, Jacob?" Cal asked again.

Jacob looked up at him, a look of anguish upon his face. He took in a deep breath before speaking.

"They...scalped her. She was trying to run away, and they shot arrows into her until she fell. Then one of them jumped from his horse..."

tears filled Jacob's eyes and he shuddered at the horrific scene he was suddenly remembering. "He scalped her. Cut her while she screamed in pain. I couldn't help her. I was too far away. I had fallen, hit my head, too late to help her when I came to my senses. Oh, God," he moaned, and he held his head within his hands and wept until he had no more tears inside of him. When at last he quieted, he looked over at Cal, a look of great sadness upon his face. "I'm sorry," he said, and he shook his head in disbelief at what he had remembered. "I couldn't help her, Cal. None of them. They rode off with all my grandchildren, leaving my daughter and her husband laying there..." again his words stopped, as he remembered. "They scalped my wife...she screamed and screamed, and I couldn't help her. Dear God, Cal. If only I hadn't fallen...I could have *done something.* Could have *tried* to help her."

Setting the coffeepot back upon the stove, giving the older man time to compose himself, Cal felt a wealth of compassion for all that Jacob Wright had been through. He'd heard stories of the brutality the Pawnee showed toward the settlers they attacked. He felt sorry for Jacob, sorry for what he'd been through. Well, he thought, it's best he remember it now, while he's here. Lord knows I can understand what he's feeling. Poor old fellow. "Jacob, let me warm up your coffee, my friend. Here." Cal added some coffee to his cup, thinking that his own hurts weren't as bad, really, as what Jacob had suffered. *His* hadn't been near as bad. At least Ophelia hadn't suffered right before his eyes, like Jacob's wife had done. He walked back over to his cot, bending first to look into the small mirror that he had replaced after breaking his other one years before. My heavens, he thought, seeing how badly he needed a shave and haircut. Glancing down at his shirt, he saw the stain on the front of it and how wrinkled it was. He looked over at the other man, seeing that he sipped slowly from his cup, his eyes filled with great sadness. He finished his coffee, stretching a bit, aware that he had been wallowing in his own grief for...how long? A month? Two weeks?

Ever since Ophelia's funeral, he thought, and he figured on his fingers how many days he'd been lost in feelings of sorrow and guilt, blaming himself for her death. He sat back down on his cot, his voice soft as he began to speak…

"Jacob, you're not alone in your grief. I've laid around here ever since Ophelia's funeral. Haven't been myself, since it. I…blamed myself for her death. I'd said something that hurt her very badly, you see. I tried to make up for it. Tried to make things right between us, but it was too late. She took sick and…well…she died, and I've hated myself for it ever since. I never meant to hurt her. She was the best wife a man could have. Just like your wife, just like her aunt Belle, she was a good woman, always doing all she could for everyone, including me. Then she overheard a foolish remark I made, when I didn't know she was around. I was talking out loud, *thinking* out loud, and things were never the same between us again. You've made me take a good look at myself, my friend. Made me see that I'm not the only one who lost someone they loved. Sometimes we get so bent low by our grief that we forget we're not the only ones hurting. I haven't even tried to comfort Ophelia's aunts. I imagine they're beside themselves with grief. It's a good thing that Belle has you to turn to. I'm glad. I guess it's time I forget what I've been feeling, and start thinking of somebody besides myself. There isn't anybody to help Aunt Hilda, as far as I know. And as prickly a gal as she is, well, I'm sure she's having a real hard time of it." He reached his hand out to Jacob. "I thank you for coming here today, my friend. You've been a great help to me and I'm grateful."

Jacob took Cal's hand, glad that remembering the tragedy that he'd been through had somehow touched Cal and brought him back from the depths. Jacob smiled at his friend. "And remember, Cal, I just might be in a position to buy the Mercantile someday, if you still want to sell it then."

"Were you serious about looking for work?" Cal asked.

"Dead serious," he said, and he gulped as he realized what he had said. "I am serious. Especially now that the lovely Belle is my wife. I'm not a slacker when it comes to work, Cal. I'd like to repay all those who've helped us, the sooner the better. If you know of a job I can do, at least until planting time, let me know."

"Well, it just so happens that I might need a man to spell me at the store a few days a week. Do you think you'd like to do that?"

"That'd be dandy," Jacob replied. "Just let me know when, and I'll be here."

"It's a deal, then," Cal said, and again he reached out and shook Jacob's hand, feeling a spark of hope rekindle inside of him. "I'm glad you came today, Jacob. I think you've saved my life, my friend."

"I'm glad," Jacob replied. "It's time we both got on with our lives, I'd say. Time we counted our blessings."

CHAPTER 19

Early the next morning, Cal walked up the front steps of the hospital. There was no sign of movement from within, nor any lights showing from the windows. He opened the door, hesitating for only a moment while he gathered himself together. He had not been in the hospital since Ophelia died, and he tried not to think of that. Walking down the hallway, he looked into each room. A patient was asleep in the first room, snoring loudly. Cal knew that there were no more cases of the Scarlet Fever that had taken not only Ophelia's life, but the lives of so many children. He also knew the hospital had been scrubbed from top to bottom in the past week, and that it was safe to be there.

As he reached the kitchen, he was surprised to find Annathea Blossom sitting at the table, an untouched cup of tea before her. Her eyes were closed, and he could see that her weathered old cheeks were wet with tears. "Aunt Hilda," he said, keeping his voice low so as not to startle her. It was a moment or two before she stirred and looked over at him.

"Cal," she said, acknowledging him, but said nothing more.

"Are you all right?" he asked. "Is there anything I can do for you?"

She did not answer, and he walked to the table, pulling out the chair closest to hers. Silence prevailed. Outside a dog barked, and the sound of someone calling a greeting to someone else could be heard, but inside the silence continued. After a few minutes, Cal stood and got himself a cup of tea, then returned to his seat at the table.

"I didn't touch any of...her things...upstairs," Aunt Hilda said at last. "Thought, since that's your room, too, I'd better leave well enough alone."

"All right," Cal replied. "I'm...sorry," he said, and his voice choked up, causing him to sit quietly, unable to say more. He sipped his tea, not really tasting it, or caring.

"The room's clean. Missus Yeager and Katie came and helped Judith and me clean. We scrubbed it down...the walls, floors, bedding. Everything," Aunt Hilda said, finally looking over at him. Her eyes widened just a tiny bit and then she said, "You look terrible."

Cal couldn't help smiling, "Yup. No wonder." Again a lengthy silence followed, as they drank their tea, both at a loss for words.

"I loved her," Cal said, at last. "I hope you know that." Again there was a long uncomfortable silence, as they both stared down into their cups, and he wished she would say something.

Aunt Hilda rose, walking over to the cupboard, her shoulders slumped as if the weight of the world rested upon them, Cal noticed. He was surprised how small she looked, how old and worn and tired. He had never noticed before, and knew that Ophelia's death had taken a terrible toll on her. "If I can do anything," he offered, not knowing what else to say. He wished she'd say something, tell him how she felt, yell at him if she must, or cry. Tell him what she thought of him, that she blamed him for Ophelia's death, *anything*...the silence that stood between them tore at him worse than any words of incrimination ever could have. When she did speak, Cal could not believe his ears.

"I blame myself," Aunt Hilda said, her voice a monotone. "It's all my fault. I should never have agreed to come here and help her make this house"—she motioned with her head toward the hall—"into a hospital. I knew it was not a proper undertaking; too much work, too many chances of catching an illness. I have no one now but *myself* to blame. Her voice rose as she continued. "I should *never* have agreed to come...or encouraged her, by doing so. I knew how she was; always such a worker, never taking time for herself, never getting enough rest or pacing herself. She was always like that, even when young. I knew that, and yet I did *nothing* to discourage her when she decided to turn this into a hospital. Why didn't I use my head? I could have said no. I should have...but when I read how happy she was, and how excited...I simply packed my belongings...and came." She put up a hand to stop Cal from interrupting. "I shall live with the knowledge the rest of my life, now. The knowledge that I, and I alone, am the reason Ophelia is... gone. I don't know how I will *ever forgive myself* Cal. As God is my witness, *I killed her*, as surely as if I stabbed her with a knife." Aunt Hilda bowed her head then, and closed her eyes, saying no more, and her grief was so strong as to be palpable.

Cal rose, removed his coat, then knelt on one knee beside her chair and slowly reached out to wrap his arms around the wizened old woman, knowing no other way to comfort her. As he did so, she turned toward him, rested her weathered cheek against his shoulder and began to sob. He held her like that all the while she cried, whispering words he hoped would console her. He was aware as he knelt there, his arms around her, that there was barely anything to her. It was as if he was holding a skeleton, and he was surprised, never having noticed before. He had always thought of her as so strong and fiesty, a "tough old bird," as he had once remarked to Ophelia, causing her to shake her finger at him and laugh. How she could blame herself, he did not know. If anyone is to blame, it is I, and I alone, he thought, and someday—if she'll listen—I'll explain this to her so she'll understand and no longer blame herself.

As she quieted, he took his arms from around her, handing her his handkerchief, then stood. She sniffled loudly, blew her nose into it two or three times, then handed it back to him. Wiping her eyes on the edge of her apron, she looked up at him. "We'll talk no more of it," she said, taking in a deep breath. "I've patients to tend to, and you've got things of your own to do, I'm sure." He nodded at her, feeling a tenderness toward her that he had never felt before. She stood, walking over to the stove, and as he lifted his coat from the back of his chair and turned to head upstairs, he heard her softly whisper, "Thank you," and it warmed his heart.

CHAPTER 20

Cal forced himself to go upstairs, his feet feeling heavier with each step. He took in a deep breath as he reached the doorway, looking into the room. The bedding had been removed from their bed, and the wardrobe doors stood open. Cal hesitated only a moment, then entered, tossed his coat on the bed, and ran a hand through his hair. He fought the thoughts that were starting to tear at him, knowing it would take little to plunge him back into sadness. Walking over to the bed, he sat down on his side, holding his head between his hands, trying to get his thoughts in order. He hated being here, hated remembering the look on Ophelia's face when she overheard him that day, hated...he stood, shaking his head, trying to shake himself free of the memories.

Entering their sitting room, he looked around at Ophelia's trinkets that lined a wooden shelf there. I need to get out of here, he thought, but instead he slumped down into the comfortable chair nearest the bedroom door. He thought then of Jacob Wright, of his visit to the Mercantile the previous day. Lord knows he's been through more than I, Cal thought. The poor fellow had lost his memory because of it, in fact. I wish I could be so lucky, he thought, and then remembered Jacob's last words to him; that they both needed to count their blessings. Yes, he supposed, there were still blessings to consider. Aunt

Hilda, for one, and the fact that she wasn't blaming *him* for Ophelia's death. He smiled as he thought of the woman who had always seemed so formidable, right from the first moment he'd been introduced to her. Feisty was not nearly a strong enough word for her, he'd always thought, until today. He sat there, remembering how hard she'd cried, laying her head against him, her body so much thinner than before. He thought of all the days the old aunt had worked right alongside of Doc, tending the fevered patients, not taking much time to sleep, or rest. Probably ate very little then, too, he supposed, aware of what a hard worker she was. Poor old gal. I wonder what she'll do, now that Ophelia's gone and Auntie Belle has married. Probably work herself to death...or grieve herself to death. He rose, walking to the window, looking out into the stillness of the early morn. I don't know how she'll stand it, he thought. I know I can't. I wish I was a million miles from here now.

His eyes stared at the snow that fell beyond the window, but suddenly he wasn't seeing it. Suddenly he was seeing, as clearly as if he was there, his land far outside of town. The beautiful hillside where he had always intended to build a home, the winding stream that led to the lake, far below. The stately oaks and pine stand off to the west, and the golden field to the east that he'd planned to plow and plant. He could see it all, as clearly as he could see the snow that fell outside the hospital window, and suddenly he knew where he wanted to be, and what he wanted to do! A smile burst upon his face, a firm conviction filling him. I'm going to build my house, he thought. I'm going to build it exactly as I always planned, on that beautiful piece of land I bought so many years ago! He turned, walking out of the room. Grabbing up his coat and pulling it quickly on, he rushed down the stairs, never looking back. I'm going *home,* he thought, and before anything or anyone could stop him, he left the hospital by the side door, feeling the first glimmer of happiness and hope he'd felt in a long time.

Jacob Wright could watch the store on the days I'm busy with the planning and building, and Aunt Hilda could tend to whatever should be done with Ophelia's clothes and such, when she was able. He smiled as he hurried down the street, unaware of the cold wind that buffeted him. He had to find the drawings he'd made so long ago, of the house he'd someday build. That 'someday' had come at last, and it would be his salvation, he was sure, as he crossed the street, his spirits higher than they'd been in years. He'd thought his dream had ended when he'd become blind in the gunfight, had given up on his dreams then. But now he knew what he had to do, and by golly, he thought, I'm not wasting anymore time! It didn't matter that he'd once intended the house to be for him and Lea. It was enough that, at long last, it would be a home for him. A home to enjoy in his old age. A home where he could watch the sun rise and set from his own front porch, and watch the deer drink from along the wooded edge of the lake. A home where he could finally feel a sense of belonging...and a sense of contentment.

CHAPTER 21

A week later, Cornelius T. Attbury was surprised when he entered the Mercantile, discovering the clerk to be an older man with full white beard. He had wanted to speak to the owner, Dunnevey. The old chap was a friendly fellow, however, and they soon got to chatting about the high cost of things, the heavy snows that blanketed the area, and how lovely South Carolina was in the spring. Cornelius was homesick for his home and family, having come to Hastings on a matter of business.

When they finished their conversation, to his surprise, the clerk—a gent named Jacob Wright—asked if he'd like a cup of coffee or tea. Cornelius was pleased to accept, having grown tired of the food at the boardinghouse across the street. It was tasteless and plain, as far as he was concerned, used to the culinary treats of the South as he was. He sat beside his new friend, sipping the hot tea, glad for the congenial conversation. He'd been in Hastings much longer than he'd intended, confined to his room at the boardinghouse with a chest cold while suffering the most terrible congestion, at first, and after, to avoid any chance of catching the Scarlet Fever that had ravaged the town. Once he had felt better, he'd been unable to discover the whereabouts of the man he sought. He'd had a long trip for nothing, and he felt disgusted with himself, knowing he'd have to return to his hometown, his business unfinished.

"Can I ask what it is that brought you to Hastings," Jacob asked, interrupting Cornelius as he sipped his tea.

"Business, sir. A most important business, in fact, pertaining to the ownership of some land in my state. I can divulge no more of the details, though I'd hoped to deliver the papers and information I carry to the rightful owner and be on my way home, post-haste. Sadly, the man has left Hastings, and I can no longer do as I'd intended."

"It must be terribly important, if you had to travel all the way here to see to it," Jacob remarked.

"Ah, yes," Cornelius replied, "that it was...or should I say, *is*. I feel I have been remiss in my duty, sadly, and now no longer know what to do, except to return home."

"Is it a settler you seek, my friend? Someone heading west, perhaps?" Jacob asked, thinking of the Indian attack upon his family, his thoughts making his stomach churn, thinking what that person might endure.

"Not a settler. No. A man who fought in the war. Fought for the South, though by birth he was a Northerner...a yankee, if I may be so blunt."

"I see," Jacob said, settling back into his chair to get more comfortable. "A shame you missed him."

"Yes, truly it is, as the information I have for him is quite favorable in nature. But, alas, I've spoken to his brother, and he said this fellow left for California a short while ago. Apparently when I was laid low by illness, and he'd not mentioned the route he'd planned to follow, nor how soon he hoped to arrive at his sister's, once there."

He put his empty cup down upon the desk, stood, stretching a bit before picking up his valise and setting his hat firmly upon his head. "It's been most enjoyable talking with you, Jacob. If you're ever in my state, do make it a point to stop and see me. I'd better get over to the boardinghouse now, though, and watch for the stage. I was told it was due at noon, and it's nearly that now. Thank you, again, for the tea and much appreciated conversation and hospitality."

Cornelius gave a slight bow of his head, shook Jacob's hand, and hurried from the store. Jacob watched him cross the street, seeing him sidestep to avoid a horse and rider that crossed his path, obviously not caring a tad if he ran the little man down, or not. He wondered who it was that his new acquaintance had good news for, not able to remember any of the folks he knew who had recently left town for California. Too bad, he thought, to have to come all this distance only to miss the man by a matter of days.

He turned, walking back to pick up the cups and take them into Cal's room at the back of the store, quickly washing them. He thought of Belle and his grandchildren, and wondered what they were doing. Jared was probably reading by the fire, he thought, and Juliana was most likely helping Mary with her spelling. And Belle, he thought, dear sweet Belle was probably working on the quilt she had started the day after they'd been married. That, or mending the pants he'd ripped the other day when he was patching the roof. He smiled, his heart filled with joy as he thought of Belle. Maybe I'll surprise her, he thought, take her a small trinket or pretty hair ribbon. Hearing the bell at the front door chime, he walked back out into the store to greet a customer, thankful for the many blessings in his life.

CHAPTER 22

The house on the hill that Cal Dunnevey built was finished just as the first flower of spring burst forth from the earth. He had hired an extra number of men to transform his drawings into the large home he had dreamed of, so many years. Some of those men wondered how he could afford so many workers, and build such a grand home, unaware that many years before Cal had sold the Mercantile at a substantial profit to Angus MacGregor, and upon MacGregor's death, it had been bequeathed back to him by MacGregor, who had become one of his best friends. Having been blind for a great number of years, Cal had not spent much of that money, and had, in fact, added to it.

The house consisted of two stories; the downstairs having a large living area, separate kitchen, and two smaller rooms, plus pantry. The upstairs consisted of three rooms; two good-sized bedrooms, and one much larger room with windows that greeted the morning sun and looked out over the lake, far below. It was this room, in particular, that drew Cal to it, the view from the windows so exceedingly magnificent. From those windows he could look out over, not only the lake to the forest far beyond, but the prairie to the east, as far as the eye could see. On days that it was too cold to sit outside on the porch, surveying his land, he would retire to this upstairs room and breathe in the view, its magnificence filling him with feelings such as he'd never experienced before. He felt as close to heaven in this grand house, as a man could feel, and wondered why it had taken him so long to build it.

Jacob Wright handled all aspects of business at the Mercantile in town, three and sometimes four days a week now, freeing Cal to not only get moved into his new home, but acquire furniture for it. Some items were ordered from as far away as in the east. To his relief—and her delight—Aunt Hilda agreed to help him acquire the needed smaller furnishings for the house, and it pleased him to see the happiness this brought her. Thinking about it, he had realized that *being needed* was what pleased her most, and thus, he had appealed to her for her help. It was apparent, almost immediately, that this assumption was correct. She walked through the house, commenting favorably on not only the layout, but the view from each of the windows, and immersed herself in the job of ordering and purchasing all he would need to make the house a home.

He had to smile as he thought of how often he'd found her sitting out on the porch, a list upon her lap, her eyes searching for sight of a deer at the edge of the lake, or watching the clouds billowing across the sky. Once in awhile he caught her crying, and knew what it was that grieved her so. He, too, had been drawn to tears on occasion, wishing that Ophelia had gotten the chance to live in this grand house and to enjoy the beauty surrounding it. But it was not to be, and they had to accept it. Life went on, in spite of the loss they'd been through with Ophelia's passing.

Now she rested at the cemetery in town, and often Cal stopped there, wishing so much that things had been different. With the building of his house, however, he'd come to accept his lack of blame concerning Ophelia's death, and found his spirits soaring with each improvement made to the house. And much to his surprise, thoughts of Lea did not enter his mind, as he had expected. All that he thought of was the house, and it soothed him in ways he had never expected, as he watched it take form. He had heard the expression that "a man's home was his castle," but had never given it much thought until the day he had stood out in front of his house, the last of the workers riding off toward their own homes, their work now finished. He'd stood there, a feeling of anticipation filling him, yet not believing his eyes. It's mine, he thought, my home! A *real* home, not a room in the back of a store, but a home of my own. He had never had a house to call his home before, having lived in an upstairs room at the saloon where his mother, Maggie, had raised him, first, and last, the rooms at the top of the stairs in the hospital with Ophelia. Removing his hat, he turned slowly in a full circle, looking out over the land—*his* land—an intense feeling of joy and contentment filling him.

"Welcome home, Calvin Dunnevey," he said aloud, and he took in a deep breath, then walked up onto the porch of his house and entered, taking his time, reverence filling him. He walked through every room, touching the cupboards, a wall, a window frame. Touching them so he would believe they were real. And still he could not believe his eyes. It was real, and it was his. Over and over he told himself that, while silently thanking God for the wealth of joy he was feeling. His mother, Maggie, would have been so happy here. Ophelia, too. For just a moment he wondered if Lea would have been. But quickly he shut the thought from his mind. Lea was gone, as surely as the other two women he had loved were gone, and it was foolish to let himself think of her.

He moved slowly through each room, his footsteps silent as he climbed the stairs. He decided to place his bed near the windows in the largest room so he could see the stars at night as he lay there. This will be my room, he thought, and he knew he'd relish every moment spent in it. A table and chairs would sit in one corner, his desk and chair along the inside wall. Here he would read his paper and do whatever paperwork he needed to, in total peace and quiet.

Walking downstairs, he went back out onto the porch, seeing in his mind two rocking chairs sitting there, facing the lake, though sitting in them one would only see a sliver of the far side of the lake and forest beyond. He leaned against the porch railing, remembering that Jonas Hart had made a pair of beautiful rocking chairs and brought them to the Mercantile just a few weeks before. Cal often sold chairs and quilts and other such things that the townsfolk made during the long winter months when they were more or less confined to their homes. Tomorrow I'll go buy both rocking chairs, he thought, and a quilt or two.

Suddenly an idea came to him that both surprised and pleased him. "I'm going to ask Aunt Hilda to come live here," he said. "She'd probably like having a real home, instead of just a room at the hospital. It must be pretty lonely for her there, now that Auntie Belle's gotten married and moved out." He stroked his chin, looking up as a flock of geese flew across the sky, their calls a satisfying music to his ears. "Yup, my mind's made up. I'll ask her tomorrow when I go into town. She's a tough old bird, but she's got a heart of gold. I'm sure she'll like it here, and I wouldn't mind her company." He yawned, stretching his arms wide, then smiled a contented smile. After all, he thought, I've grown fond of the old gal, in spite of how ornery she can be.

CHAPTER 23

Eli Hart rode through town, glad to be away from the farm. All week he'd felt a restlessness grow within him, and though he'd fought it, it had kept at him until he'd decided he needed to get away. A case of 'spring fever' Lilly had explained when he'd told her at breakfast how he felt. In fact, it was she who had suggested he ride out to visit her sister, Lydia, and Michael. "After all," she'd said, "it'll soon be time to plow and plant, and then you won't have the chance to get away." He'd asked Jonas if there was anything he needed help with, and the older man had smiled, telling him he'd manage, as he nodded toward the door. He smiled, thinking of Jonas, knowing that somehow he had always seemed to understand him. He'd been a good father, one of the best, and Eli was proud to think of himself as his son. I've had two good fathers, he thought, and he remembered back to the day he'd found out that his friend, Michael, was not only a friend, but was in actuality his *real* father. He'd been furious, finding this out, and had set out for the hospital where Michael was recovering from a wound upon his neck. Not realizing that Michael, too, had only recently discovered the truth. He had railed at him, upbraiding him for keeping the truth from him and eventually stormed from the hospital, riding off, his temper driving him on. Johnny Gentry had seen how angry he was, and being the true friend he was, had followed Eli, talking to him and causing him to rethink the situation, once they'd stopped riding.

Eli ran a hand through his hair, waving at Katie Yeager as she walked with her mother toward their store, his thoughts going from that day to Johnny. He wondered where Johnny was and if he was all right. It had been so long since he'd seen him, and word of mounting troubles between the white settlers and the Indians were not favorable. Things had gotten far out of hand, in fact, after that soldier, Custer, had gone into the Black Hills sending word of the discovery of gold there. After that, whites by the number had stormed to the area, greed driving them, with no thought given to any of the treaties stating that the Black Hills were property of the Indians, and whites were not to go there. Reports of attacks on Indian camps by soldiers had come, and Eli had listened, fearing for his friend. He knew Standing Elk's camp had been in the same area, and he hoped that no harm had come to either Johnny, or his mother, who had chosen to live with the Indians.

He nodded at the blacksmith as he passed by, not in any hurry to head for Michael's. The sun warmed his back, and though there was an occasional bit of snow that had not completely melted away, it was a swell day to be out and about. The road through town had not turned to a sea of muddy ruts, as the ground still was frozen, and he rode slowly along, enjoying the sights and sounds around him. Hastings had grown these past years, what with so many more boats on the river, each bringing more passengers to town. And the train station was filled with even more passengers, more arriving, than leaving. There was a millinery shop now next to the Yeager's store, a small newspaper next to the Mercantile, and the jail took up nearly twice as much room as it had the summer before, Eli noticed. More cells, he thought, to keep up with the influx of drunks and rowdies, robbers and roughians arriving daily. He pulled up at the Lucky Lady, thinking a drink would quench the thirst he felt. Entering, he was surprised to recognize the fellow he and Johnny had seen ages ago, though his hair was mostly white, and his girth had grown. Jasper...Jared...what was his name, Eli thought. He racked his brain, trying to remember, ordering a whiskey as he did so. The bartender made small talk as he poured Eli's drink, then looked down the bar, asking, "You want another, Jubal?" The old man nodded, a toothless grin crossing his face. He wiped his nose on his sleeve, taking some money from his pocket, eyeing Eli closely as he did so.

"Don't I know ya, son?" he asked, studying Eli, his dark beard showing the remains of a meal he'd eaten.

"Suppose so," Eli answered, wishing the man's memory wasn't so good.

The man continued to study him, clearing his throat as he did so, and spitting toward a spittoon that sat nearby. He missed, but that didn't bother him. Again he wiped his nose on his already filthy sleeve and squinted his eyes at Eli, intent on remembering. Eli wished he had not come into the saloon. It was something he'd rarely done, and he'd only done so today because he'd been at the farm so long, and wanted to partake of the activities going on in the saloon. He liked the music of the old piano, and watching the expressions on the faces of the men playing cards—the stakes sometimes quite high—and the girls, with their fancy dresses and welcoming smiles. More than once he had enjoyed their company, over the years, as all young men often did. He finished his drink, paying for it, then turned to leave.

"I know where I seen ya," Jubal said, stopping Eli with these words. "Seen ya on my way inta town, you and that injun kid...Sheriff Gentry's kid. Remember? The day he took that there necklace off'n me. What'd he call it? A...medal...*medallion*, that's what he said. Claimed it was his pa's, though I got my doubts. Ya remember?"

"I remember," Eli stated, turning back to face the old man. "It was his pa's. I recognized it, too."

"Well, that's what you say, so's I guess it was," Jubal said. Eli turned away, not caring to hear anymore. "Too bad about that young fella. But, what can ya expect, raised to like them redskins like he was, and him havin' the same blood. I ne'er knew 'bout that 'til I seen the kid." He shook his head, hacking and spitting in the direction of the spittoon once more. Eli looked away, knowing he was far off his mark again.

"What did you mean when you said, too bad about that young fella?" Eli asked, his attention focusing squarely on the old man.

"I guess you ain't heard," Jubal Cade said, looking at Eli. "I done some trappin' near old Standing Elk's camp. A peaceable old feller he was, not like them Pawnee. They'll scalp ya for no good reason at all. But Standing Elk weren't like that. He'd welcome ya into his village, sharing the pipe and all. I liked him. Smart he was, too. 'bout as smart as any white man I ever talked to. He said that white woman that lived with 'em—she was that kid's maw, ya know—she taught him to understand the whites, taught 'em to speak our language, so's they'd know what we was saying..." he stopped talking and took a large swig of his whiskey, emptying the glass, then motioned to Eli that he'd like another. Eli nodded toward the bartender, waiting for the old fellow to continue. "Well, like I said, he was smart. Sneaky, too, not telling the whites he could understand them, ya know." He shook his head, while Eli waited, his patience running thin. Jubal took up his glass, swilling down another drink, then continued. "I was up there, near their camp, tracking a bunch of wolves. Their pelts bring some good money, ya see, and low and behold I come upon these soldiers, all hidden fer the night in a gulley awful close to the camp. I was surprised to see 'em, and thought maybe they'd share a bite with me. But then I seen how quiet they was being, and realized they was up to no good. Weren't sure about it, at first, but about the time I got close enough to 'em, they headed out, quiet as could be, and then I see what they got a mind to do. I couldn't do nothing to help, ya see—being too far from the old chief's camp—so I stayed where I was, thinking it was safer to be there, and that they'd not be too happy to know I'd seen what they done." He reached for his glass, but Eli stopped him.

"Git on with what you were saying," Eli ordered. "What about Johnny?"

"Don't know 'bout him. Never found his body, ya see. But I seen his mother...beautiful woman she was...and that's the truth. Why she'd choose to stay with them Indians...well, that's beside the point now. The soldier in charge killed her, slicing away at her with his saber, first thing. I seen it all. The chief and some of his braves had ridden out to get some meat, ya see, and that soldier—the one with the white hair—led his men into the camp, shouting and shooting! I tell ya, I never seen anything like it! Them Indians never had a chance. He cut yer friend's maw down quick as could be, whilst his men rode through camp butchering all the rest of 'em, even the old, and young uns and babies. 'Bout made me sick, it did, and I hid. Didn't dare let them see me, knowing what I'd seen. Later, I snuck into Standing Elk's camp, *not taking anything,* mind ya. But looking around, wondering what had made that soldier hate that woman and them Injuns so."

"You never saw Johnny among the dead?" Eli asked, his upset apparent.

"No sir. He weren't among 'em. Mighta been out hunting with them other braves, though. I didn't stick around long enough to see. I saw a man riding fast as the wind toward the camp, and I lit out as fast as my horse could take me. Didn't want that fella to think I was to blame, ya see." He motioned toward his glass, a questioning look upon his face. Then he turned and spit, once more missing his target, before asking, "How 'bout another drink, son?" But when he turned back, Eli was already hurrying from the saloon.

129

CHAPTER 24

Jumping on his horse, the reins held tightly in his hands, Eli spurred the horse and raced through town, to the surprise of the folks who saw him. He bent low over his horse's neck, racing as if the devil himself was after him. Sheriff MacKay looked up as Eli raced by, not certain what had caused the panicked look on the young man's face. He wondered if something had happened at the Lucky Lady Saloon, and thought he had better mosey on down there and ask. He'd seen the Hart kid go into the saloon, earlier, but hadn't heard any shots. Maybe there was a fight, he thought, checking his gun and pulling on his hat.

Eli clung to his horse, urging it on, not taking time to think out what he would do, or where he would go. All he knew was that Johnny was his best friend, and he had to know if he was all right. Racing like the wind, he attempted to pull his coat more tightly around him, but was unable to with only one hand, the other holding firm to the reins. I'll get more bullets from Michael, he thought, and borrow a blanket. He wasn't even sure just where Standing Elk's camp was, knowing it lay in Sioux territory, a far distance from where he was now. In his mind he pictured the scene that Jubal Cade had described: the white-haired soldier striking Sarah down with his sword, her, the elders and the children, some mere babies. Anger raged within him at these thoughts. He knew of Standing Elk from stories Johnny had told him. Knew that his were a peaceable people, not given to causing trouble. How many nights had he and Johnny sat talking; Johnny telling him of the kindness and wisdom of the old chief, and the stealth with which his father's best friend, Howling Wolf, had hunted. Howling Wolf had even taught Johnny's father, Moses, the Indian way of hunting, and Eli had learned much as he listened, and was impressed.

As he neared Michael's cabin, he pulled up, jumping from his horse. He raced up to the door, pounding on it, while glancing at the barn, wondering if Michael was inside it. But just as he began to turn from the door it was opened by a startled looking Lydia. "Eli. What's wrong? Is it Lilly?" she asked, placing one hand upon her heart. Eli brushed by her, saying no, and asking where Michael was.

"Why, he's out in the pasture...checking fences," she said. "Please, son, tell me what's wrong?"

"I just got word in town that Sarah Gentry is dead, killed by a soldier. Most of the tribe's been wiped out, though I'm not sure about Johnny. I have to go find out. He might be hurt, might need me." Eli walked over to where Michael stored his supply of bullets, reaching to fill his pockets.

"I'll go get your father," Lydia said, so upset that she could not think clearly. "Wait here," she said. But Eli grabbed her arm, telling her there wasn't time. She stood, her heart pounding, not knowing just what to do. "You can't go alone," she said, at last, already aware that he would not listen. "Please, Eli. Wait until I go get your father," she pleaded. But Eli was already heading for the door.

"Tell Michael I couldn't wait," he said, turning to face her. "I'm sorry, Lydia...Mother, but I can't wait. Johnny might be hurt. I need to go now. Tell Michael to ride out to the farm and tell my ma and pa what's happened. Tell them not to worry. I'll come back as soon as I can." He paused, looking around the room. "Do you have a blanket I can borrow?" he asked. Lydia rushed to get the blanket off the bed, then grabbed up some food: apples, coffee, dried meat, and such, and a few other necessary items her son might need. Taking them from her— anxious to be on his way—he hurried to his horse, filling the saddlebags. He'd decide the best course of action to take, later, when he stopped for the night. But right now, all he could think of was Sarah Gentry, lying dead, and knew if Johnny had been there, there was a good chance that he had also been killed, or wounded. He would not—*could not*—rest until he knew for sure. As long as they'd been friends, they had always stood together. Any battle Johnny fought had been his battle, too. This time would not be any different. Johnny was more a brother than a friend, always had been, and Eli's loyalty to his friend drove him on.

He finished stuffing his saddlebags, then turned to Lydia. She stood there, tears streaming from her eyes, as he reached out to wrap his strong arms around her. "I'll be back," he said, wishing he could tell her how glad he was that they had gotten to know each other. "Don't worry, Mother," he said, as she clung to him, her sobs muffled by his coat. "Tell Michael to go to the farm. Don't forget. I love you," he stated, pulling away from her, swinging up onto the saddle.

Lydia watched him ride away, sick with worry. "I love you, too," she called out, not knowing if he had heard, or not, as he raced toward the forest and quickly disappeared from sight.

CHAPTER 25

Michael heard Lydia's sobs as he walked up the path to their cabin about fifteen minutes later. He paused, thinking at first that it was a bird he was hearing. But when he realized the sound was coming from the cabin, he rushed inside, worry showing upon his face. Lydia sat at the table, her head resting in her arms, her sleeve wet from the tears she had shed. "Lydia," he said, hurrying to her side. "What is it, honey? What's happened?" She looked up at him, then burst into more crying, unable to control herself. "Tell me what's wrong," Michael insisted, pulling her up to stand before him, placing his arms around her. When she answered, he felt weak in the knees from worry.

"It's Eli," she said, when she could quiet herself enough to speak. "He's gone, Michael. Oh, Michael, our boy's *gone?* and again she burst into tears.

"Gone where?" Michael demanded, shaking her gently by the shoulders. "Gone where?"

"He came, took some of your bullets, and food," she said. "He said he heard in town that Sarah Gentry had been killed, her and the Indians. Killed by soldiers, he said, and he said he didn't know if Johnny was dead or alive, but that he might be wounded, and he had to go find him." She was shaking as she told him, and he walked her over to their bed and sat beside her on it, his arm around her. "He wants you to go to Lilly's. Said to tell her and Jonas where he's gone, and that..." she started to cry again. "That he'll come back as soon as he can. Oh, Michael, what should we do? What if we lose him? What if he gets killed?"

Michael felt the same fear that she did, his mind whirling as he tried to decide what to do. "When did he leave?" he asked, rising and heading for the door.

"Not long ago," she said. "Only a few minutes ago."

"Which way did he go? Maybe I can catch him, stop him," Michael said, loading his gun and shoving it into his holster.

"To the north, toward the forest," Lydia said, rushing to open the door for her husband. "Hurry, Michael. Please hurry."

A few minutes later Michael's horse raced from the barn, and she watched her husband spur the animal, racing toward the forest. She clasped her hands together, whispering a prayer that he would catch up with their boy and talk him into turning back. The stories she had heard of late, of the battles taking place between the whites and the Indians filled her heart with fear for Eli. Settlers were being killed every day, wagon trains discovered, bodies laying beside them, children and women sometimes stolen, men killed, many scalped. Every story filled her with dread as the war between the two peoples became more and more deadly. And now their son was riding right into Indian territory in hope of finding his friend. Lydia took in a deep breath, numbed by fear for their son. "He will come back," she told herself, willing herself to believe it. "He *will* come back. He has to. Dear God, *he has* to!"

CHAPTER 26

It was nearly dark when Jonas heard someone coming down the lane to the farm. He thought at first that it was Eli, then realized it wasn't a horse and rider, but instead a horse and buggy. He put down his paper and stood, stretching a bit, then walked over to look out the window. He was surprised when he saw that it was Michael and Lydia, and when he saw the looks on their faces his heart jerked inside his chest. "What is it?" he asked, opening the door, lowering his voice so Lilly would not be wakened. He could see that Lydia had been crying, and that Michael was more than a little upset. "Is it the boy? What's happened?" he asked again, taking Lydia's coat and motioning her to a chair. He felt his heart begin to race and put one hand upon his chest. "Tell me," he demanded, "is it our boy?"

Michael looked at him, wanting to say "No. It's not *your* boy," but he saw the look of dread on Jonas's face and answered simply, "Yes."

Jonas sank down in a chair across from them, the color draining from his face. "Tell me what's happened," he said, never taking his eyes off Michael. He couldn't help noticing the resemblance between Eli and Michael; the tiny nerve that jumped at one side of their face when they were upset, the shape of their faces, and identical shade of their hair. He took in a deep breath, waiting for Michael to speak.

He came to the house today. He'd stopped in town, found out that Sarah Gentry had been killed; her and the Indians she stayed with, Michael said, at last. "Eli told Lydia it was a soldier who struck her down, while his troops butchered all the Indians in camp, even the babies. Eli said he didn't know if Johnny was dead or alive, said he had to go find out. Lydia tried to talk him out of it, told him to wait and talk to me, but he was all upset. He grabbed up the extra bullets I had, got a blanket and some food and lit out to find Johnny. Lydia says he wasn't even sure where the Indian camp was, but that didn't stop him none." He paused, giving Jonas a chance to speak. When he didn't, Michael continued, "I was out checking fences, got back to the cabin soon after. I went looking for him, but couldn't pick up his trail. Thought I had, but then I lost it. When I returned to the cabin, I harnessed up the buggy, and here we are."

Jonas nodded at him, still not saying anything. They noticed the quiet fortitude of the large man, and though he said nothing, they knew he was as worried as they were. Just then Lilly came down the stairs, having heard their voices. When Lydia saw her, she ran to her sister, throwing her arms about her, sobs bursting from her. Jonas moved quickly, hurrying to his wife's side, his concern for her more than evident.

"What is it?" Lilly asked, pulling free of Lydia, looking from one to the other. "What's happened?" She turned her head, looking at her husband. Reaching out toward him she asked, "Jonas, tell me what's happened. Lydia, stop bawling and get control of yourself. Why do you all look like you've lost your best friend?" And then realization hit her! The *only one* they *all* cared about, who was not present, was Eli. She moved toward Jonas, barely able to speak, "Eli?" she asked, her face paling as he nodded. Jonas put an arm around her, worried, knowing she had not been well for a long, long time.

"He's alive," he said, though his words sounded stilted, even to him. "It's just that..." he began, and slowly he repeated everything that

Michael had told him, once Lilly had taken a seat. News of Sarah's death shocked Lilly, and she had all she could do not to cry out. It took all of her strength; keeping her composure, forcing herself to remain still, wanting—more than anything—to hear the news of Eli.

Lilly listened as Jonas continued, then turned her head to where Lydia sat, crying. She noticed how red Michael's face was, and could not help but notice the look of worry upon her own husband's face. Keeping her voice as calm as possible, she said, "Eli was always close to Johnny. This doesn't surprise me in the least. He isn't a child, you know. He's a man. He's always been a loyal friend, and steadfast in his friendship with Johnny. What are you thinking, Jonas?"

"It won't do to follow him. He's set in his ways," Jonas said, running a hand through his hair. "He is a man now, young, but smart. I can understand the way he feels. He and Johnny have been as close as brothers ever since they were young. It's no different, Michael, than when your brother, Colin, heard you...ah...had some troubles, and lit out to help you. Eli feels it's his responsibility to find Johnny. I'll admit this isn't a good time for a man—a *white* man—to be heading through Indian territory, but Eli's no fool. I think the best thing we can do is to pray for his safe return and trust the Lord to get him home."

Michael looked about to say something, but nodded, instead. He was surprised at how calm Lilly was, her reaction was not at all what he had expected. He studied her, seeing how tired she looked. And yet she had taken their news about Eli as though she had no qualms, at all. It's because she *knows* Eli, he thought, because she's raised him all these years, ever since his birth. Whereas Lydia and I *barely* know him. We don't have that inner knowledge of our boy; how he thinks, how he feels. As he thought these things, he looked toward Jonas, aware that this giant of a man felt as much love for Eli as he did. It was as clear as the nose on his face. Michael looked away from Jonas, to Lydia, surprised by these realizations.

"Would you like some coffee or tea?" Lilly asked, getting to her feet. "I have a fresh cobbler to go with it. Jonas? Michael?"

"Good idea," Jonas replied, smiling at her.

Michael nodded, and Lydia rose, following her sister to the kitchen.

"Lilly," Lydia said, as soon as they were in the other room. "How can you be so calm? Aren't you afraid for Eli? I don't know how you can be so...strong."

Lilly set about making a pot of coffee, then walked to the table. Taking up a spoon, she dished up four helpings of the warm cobbler she'd made earlier that evening. She had planned to serve it when Eli returned from town. She finished, then sat in the chair nearest Lydia. Reaching out to take her hand, she gathered her thoughts, knowing the distress her younger sister was feeling, not wanting to add to it. At last she spoke; "I always knew the day would come when Eli would set off on his own...marry, perhaps, and move away. It's just something a parent expects. I didn't expect *this* to happen, of course, didn't expect him to ride off like this, in search of his friend." She paused, gazing across the room, considering her words before she spoke. "Horrible thing, these days, the wars going on between the whites and Indians. I feel for all of them. I've never understood war, Lydia. I still remember when Jonas came home from war: how ravaged he was, in body and spirit."

She got up, taking four cups from the cupboard, filling them. "I hate war, always have and always will." She paused a moment, then said, "Let's take the coffee and cobbler in to the men while it's hot, then we can talk more." They took their husbands a coffee and bowl of warm cobbler, noticing the peaceful conversation they now shared. Excusing themselves, the women headed back to the kitchen. When they were settled, Lilly continued, "Eli does have a good head on his shoulders, Lydie. He's not one to...*usually*...run off without a plan, or a purpose. The fact that he did so, tells me not only how worried he is about Johnny, but also how deeply caring he is. That quality is rarely seen in one so young, and speaks volumes. He doesn't make brash decisions—under normal circumstances—and I'm sure that when he stops for the night, he'll spend most of it deciding upon a sensible plan of action." She paused to sip her coffee, smiling at her younger sister. "Try not to worry, Lydie. Pray that he returns to us in good health, not only safe, but having found Johnny the same."

Lydia took a bite of the cobbler, followed by a swallow of her coffee, looking over at her sister. She wondered how she could be so strong. Inside, her heart fluttered wildly, every time she thought of what Eli might be facing, and without warning her eyes threatened to fill with tears. She felt—as she always had around Lilly—like a little girl; a frightened, insecure little girl who lacked the strength of her older sibling. "I don't know how you do it, Lilly," she said at last. "I don't understand how you can be so...calm. I feel so frightened, so afraid, like a child."

Lilly reached over, pushing a lock of her sister's hair back from her face. She saw the pleading look upon Lydia's face, saw, too, the toll the years had taken—because of the life she had once lived—and in that moment, Lilly realized that all the anger she had felt toward Lydia, for so long, was gone. This was her sister sitting before her, and what they shared *now* was more than they had *ever* shared before...for now they shared the boy Lydia had entrusted into her care. "I'm not as strong as you think, Lydie, not at all." She placed her hand upon her sister's, a tender smile upon her face. "It's just that I love my *son...our son...so* very much. I *have to believe* he'll be all right. He *will be!*"

Lydia turned her hand so that she now cradled Lilly's hand within hers, saying, "I'm *glad* our boy had you for his mother, Lilly. *I'm so very glad!*" And tears of healing traced a path down both women's faces.

CHAPTER 27

Later that night, after Michael and Lydia had left for their home, Lilly and Jonas made their way up to their bedroom. When ready for bed, they knelt together as they had done so many times before, and prayed. They prayed for Eli's safe return, and that he would find his friend, Johnny Gentry, and that Johnny would be alive and well. Then they prayed for peace to come for not only the settlers who, more and more, streamed into the land to the west, but for the Indians who had lived upon that land for generations. When her knees would tolerate no more kneeling, Lilly stood, patting Jonas on his shoulder, then slipped into their bed. He smiled at her, finished his prayers and supplications and quickly joined her.

Once settled and comfortable, he lay there, his thoughts many. At last he asked, "Lil, are you all right?"

She turned toward him. "I have to believe that he will return to us, Jonas, or I'm afraid I'd go mad."

He rolled over to face her, seeing her profile in the sparse light from the window. "Eli learned about tracking from Johnny. Do you remember how they'd go off by themselves, when younger? At supper he'd come in, all excited, telling us how he could track like an Indian. Remember?" He paused, his thoughts of the years, long before, when

Eli was just a boy. "Remember the day you found them out beside the barn, throwing a knife at the target they'd drawn on it? You were sure that they'd get hurt, and told them to stop, immediately." He laughed softly, and she placed her hand upon his chest, comforted by the memories he spoke of. "He'll be all right, Lil. I believe that. He's got the skills to survive in the wilds...knows all the things that Johnny taught him, plus what we've taught him. He'll be all right." He placed his large hand over hers, stretching out one leg, moving so his body settled into the mattress where it was accustomed to being.

"I hope you're right," she said, but her thoughts were far away, in another time. She was remembering the day that Sarah—then Sarah *Justus*—had come to visit. She had asked her to come, telling her she needed to discuss a 'personal matter' with her. That was the day that she'd told Sarah she loved Jonas, she remembered, and she smiled in the dark, knowing that had been the day their friendship had begun. She had always admired Sarah for her strength of character, and her fortitude. Sarah wasn't like the other girls in town, silly things such as they were. They thought only of catching some young man's eye and marrying, or of fancy dresses, or the next picnic or ice cream social, where they could bat their eyes to attract the attention of the fellow they'd set their sights on. No, Lilly thought, Sarah wasn't like that. Like me, Sarah had other values. True values. She'd learned to hunt and track from her friend, John Bruce; the old fellow she'd become so attached to as a child. He'd taught Sarah the same skills that Johnny had taught Eli, she thought, and she smiled, realizing this, thinking; if Sarah could survive alone and in the wilds, so will Eli. She snuggled closer to Jonas, taking care not to wake him, her thoughts continuing.

Sarah had looked so pretty that day, her hair done up, the dress she wore complimenting her features...the dress was blue, I think. Lilly closed her eyes, trying to remember. They'd sat out on the porch in the rocking chairs, and Sarah had commented on them. I told her Jonas had made them, and one thing led to another, and that's when I told her I loved him...had, ever since he'd first come to my folk's farm, years before. Sarah had guessed, just by our conversation, that I loved him. In fact, she'd listened to all I said—and *didn't* say—then asked, out of the clear blue, "Does he love you, too?" I'd been so shocked that she'd guessed my feelings, but she explained that I "got a look on my face" every time I mentioned his name.

Lilly smiled broadly. She thought of how shocked her friend had been when she admitted that Jonas had no idea how she felt. Her smile faded quickly as she remembered why he had not known...because of her mother, because of her illness. All those years, Lilly thought, all the years I took care of Mother. Every day after Lydia was born. No time for a life of my own, then, or the camaraderie of others my age, no picnics or parties or socials for me. Every day was the same as the one before; cooking, cleaning, doing the farm's books, and tending to mother's needs. And, as if that wasn't enough, tending to the raising of Lydia, who fought me every step of the way, being so terribly headstrong.

Lilly sighed, pained by these memories. It wasn't until much later that I told Sarah the truth. Told her that my mother was ill, and that Father, being of a gentle nature, had left after she tried to kill him as he slept one night. Sarah hadn't been the least bit upset or shocked. She had listened, understanding all that I'd been through and why, and was never lax in her friendship with me, after.

Lilly turned over, placing her feet against the back of her husband's legs to warm them, her thoughts soon continuing...And now, Sarah's dead, killed not by the Indians that everyone speaks of so viciously nowdays, but by a cavalry soldier—a white man. Lilly felt tears well-up in her eyes, but wiped them away as quickly as they came. She felt great sorrow from the loss of her friend, yet knew that Sarah wouldn't have changed her life one bit, for anything, or anyone. She had fallen in love with Gray Eagle in spite of her father's hatred for Indians, and her love for him had carried over, after his death, to his people. I can certainly understand that, Lilly thought, remembering how folks had seemed so surprised when she and Jonas had married. Even Father was surprised, me small in stature and Jonas such a great tall giant of a man. Even Father saw only the size and strength of Jonas, never seeing his gentleness or his kindly ways.

Lilly smiled, pleasant thoughts filling her mind. Sarah had understood, though, being in love, herself, with a man who lived so far outside the customary conventions of the times. She understood that it was far more important to "see" with your heart, and that is what we both did. I'm certain that she, like I, had no regrets in doing so.

Lilly shifted, once more, not able to get comfortable. Her thoughts drifted to how badly she'd felt the day her father had left. He'd returned after her mother died, and she'd been so happy to see him. But the man she had known as a child, was no longer the same man then. He'd lived away so long, had changed, had made a life for himself elsewhere. It wasn't very long before he'd come to her at her husband's farm. He'd told her then that he could not stay, to do what she wished with their family farm, that being there brought him only sad memories. And soon after, he'd left to resume the life he'd made for himself, a life without her and Lydia.

She hadn't understood, then, had been very angry at him for leaving. Later, two days before Christmas—the same year she'd fallen and lost their baby—Jonas had come from town with a letter. It was from a woman by the name of Bess. Its message was short and to the point, and appeared totally devoid of feeling. Lilly's eyes filled with tears as she remembered. She'd had a terrible feeling, upon seeing the letter, almost as if she *knew—even* before she read it—that it brought sad news. Opening it, she saw the torn piece of paper that simply said, "To the daughters of Chalmers Benedict. I regret to inform you that your father passed away the morning of..." Tears fell upon her cheeks at the memory. The letter had stated that he'd been buried in the town cemetery where he had lived, that he'd left nothing of consequence; only a few meager belongings, and was signed by the woman named Bess, nearly every word misspelled, including her father's name.

Lilly sniffled, shivering slightly. It wasn't often that she let herself think of either her father, or his passing, and remembering the letter brought her the same feeling of numbing sadness as it had the day so long ago. She'd learned that day to steel herself against the blows that life wrought. Had learned to harden herself against pain and suffering, to brace herself for whatever grief and sadness might come her way. Lord knows I've had my share, she thought, of both. Lydia thinks I'm so strong. If she only knew. My heart aches for Sarah, dear, dear Sarah. I hope she didn't suffer long. But I've learned that in this life we must be strong of spirit and never falter in our determination to persevere.

Death is a part of life. A part that can so easily knock us down, if we let it. Thinking this, she remembered how devastated she'd been after the loss of their baby, how she had not been able to sleep or eat, and had become nearly unable to function. Only the dreadful memory of Mother's insanity, brought me back to my senses, so great was my fear of becoming like her, Lilly remembered, and she pulled the quilt up around her, shivering. I was not strong then, she thought, but I had to overcome my grief. Though it's different, when the loss is a child. She thought then of Eli, of how he had gone, giving her no chance to say goodbye. No chance to tell him she loved him, though she felt certain that he knew. If only I could have told him, once more, she thought. Wiping away all trace of tears from her cheeks, she took in a deep breath, then whispered softly, "I *will not* lose *this* child. He *will* come home. I *know* he will." And she closed her eyes, hoping sleep would come.

CHAPTER 28

Questioning myself has become a habit, Eli Hart thought, as he lay on his back, watching the stars overhead. He couldn't help wonder if he'd been a fool to head out to find Johnny. He'd been riding near on to four weeks now—a whole month—with no definite destination in mind. Only the hope of finding his friend drove him on, never having realized just how vast a country it was. He'd been drenched by sudden storms, soaked to the skin and near frozen, and whipped by winds that stung his face and blinded his eyes. At night he had holed up in any shelter he could find, or faced the elements, wrapped in his blanket, praying it would stop raining.

A shooting star raced overhead, and he smiled, knowing his journey still had not been all bad. He had, afterall, gotten away from the farm for awhile. He'd had the worst case of "spring fever," as his ma called it. This year had been the worst ever. Winter had dragged on and on and seemed like it would never end. He'd mended tack and done all the other things around the farm that he could do, finally deciding a trip to town was what he needed, never dreaming he'd run into that old man at the Lucky Lady.

He snorted, remembering how Jubal had spit in the direction of the spittoon, never once hitting it. Disgusting old fool, he thought, stretching out his legs. But who am I to call *him* a fool. He's probably still at the Lucky Lady, snuggled up with one of the pretty gals, his belly full of whiskey, and here I am, out in the middle of nowhere with no idea which way to go next.

He smiled, his thoughts turning to cheerier times. He thought of how he and Johnny had once been the worst of enemies, always fighting each other when they were mere sprouts. Then that day when that kid had called him a bastard, and without thinking he'd lambasted him one. That's when things had changed. He couldn't help but grin at remembering. He probably would have killed me, Eli thought, remembering how mad the bully had gotten after he slugged him. But Johnny had come over to stand beside me, telling him he'd have to fight *both* of us, and to our great relief he swore and stormed away, vowing to settle with us later. Of course when I asked Johnny why he'd stood up to that kid with me, he'd said it was because he didn't want to see him get the best of me. Eli smiled. As if he could have, he thought. But he knew that as skinny as he'd been back then, there was a good chance that the bully would have busted him up pretty darn good if Johnny *hadn't* stepped in.

His thoughts turned then to the time he'd ridden into town, only to find a group of angry men beating the living daylights out of Johnny. Like so many then, they hated Indians, and the fact that Johnny looked like one was all they'd needed to spur them into action. I had no choice but to jump in and rescue him, Eli thought, remembering how sore his ribs had been after. He hadn't been near as bad off, though, as the old man who had also jumped in to help...that old Pearly fellow. He'd died not long after, Eli heard, and he remembered how Johnny wouldn't just leave him there in the jail, but had to wait until the doctor came and checked out the old man. That led to them having to carry him over to the hospital so the doctor could tend him. And that's when I made a darned fool of myself, ranting and raving at Michael, because I thought he'd known all along that he was my real father.

Eli turned on his side, trying to get more comfortable, his thoughts continuing. He'd made a scene that day, and it still embarrassed him to think of it; had stormed out of the hospital—mad as hell—-and raced off, angrier than he'd ever been, Johnny right behind him. Again he smiled. He knew I would eventually stop, knew I'd need to talk out my anger. Smart, too; telling me how lucky I was to have grown up thinking of Michael as one of my best friends. Johnny had lost his pa, Moses Gentry, when he was a young boy, when his pa went off to war and never returned. I had to admit—once I'd cooled down a bit—that he was right; I really was lucky to have shared a friendship with Michael.

Eli closed his eyes, wishing sleep would come, but after awhile he gave up and laid there, listening to the night sounds. It was peaceful laying there. Nocturnal animals scurried here and there as they hunted for food, and in the distance he heard a wolf howl, answered quickly by another. When the prairie grasses rustled nearby, Eli raised his head and listened, wondering what it was that passed so near. But he rested easy—taking his cue from his horse. It glanced in the direction of the sound, then went back to eating. It would have reacted differently if there was danger.

He had lain awake many nights, listening, as he was now. Spoiled by the luxury of having a comfy bed at the farm, he had been convinced, at first, that he would never adjust to the hardness of the ground, but he had. After a few nights, it had gotten much easier to sleep on it, somehow. Or was it that his body had grown harder, he wondered, even though the ground was no softer? Of course the prairie grasses made a more favorable bed than the hard ground, *that* he had to admit. Why I've even grown accustomed to riding, day after day, and aren't saddle sore, anymore. He had not given these things any thought before, having spent the majority of his life on the farm. Used to riding into town, or out to Michael's—at most—he hadn't realized how sore a fellow's butt could get, or how his legs would stiffen up from being on a horse day after day.

Lessons, he thought. I'm learning some things I wouldn't have learned if I'd stayed on the farm, and he was pleased at realizing this. Just two days past, when he had come upon that old trapper's cabin hidden well back in that grove of trees, he had learned a few things about Indians, too, that he'd not known before. Learned that it was a sign of friendship to smoke the pipe with them, *if* they offered. The old man explained that you had to be sure they were one of the *peaceable* tribes, first, otherwise you'd end up like him. And he'd removed his old coonskin hat to reveal his bald head—the skin patchy and flesh uneven—result of the scalping he'd gotten. He'd laughed uproariously, slapping his knee, after he'd said that, and Eli had almost lost his breakfast, seeing it. He hoped he wouldn't suffer a similar fate.

The old fellow seemed in awful good spirits, considering. Said he was friends with all the tribes, the peaceful ones, that is. But that he'd gotten too confident of that fact, and *careless*, and it had cost him his scalp. Eli had laughed as he told of his adventures and how he'd ended up there. He'd been hitched, he said, to a squaw by the name of Marketa— Sparkling Eyes, in our language. A pretty thing she was, he'd said, with big brown eyes and smart ways. She'd taught him a lot about surviving in the wilderness, and about the Indian people. She was Cherokee, and he stared off into the distance when he said that, Eli remembered. Come to find out, the old fellow had been a traveling preacher, many years before. A preacher, he told Eli, who had come west to 'save the Indians from their evil ways.' He laughed so hard when he said that, that drool ran down into his whiskers and his face turned fire-red. "Damnation, boy!" he'd exclaimed, when he could breathe again. "It weren't *them* that *needed* to be saved! No siree! Weren't them a'tall."

Eli had finished his bowl of gruel and sat there, enjoying the warmth of the fire and the tale the old fellow was telling. "They had their *own* beliefs, ya see. Believed that Wankan Tanka would watch o'er them. Prayed—in their own fashion—for the animal that gave them meat, and thanked the tree that gave them their bow. I knowed as soon as I seen their ways, that they had a special kind of religion. A kind that most white folk had no idea of. Why *they* weren't the ones invading the land, killing off the buffalo for the fun of it—what kind o' sense does that make, I ask ya? And lookie what it's come to now—more and more settlers comin' every day—more fellas heading to Californie, looking for gold. It's a durn shame, son. A durn shame." Eli thought now of all the old fellow had said, wishing more white men felt the same. When the old man stopped talking and took the time to light his pipe, Eli asked if he knew of Standing Elk, and where his camp was. The old fellow eyed him suspiciously, it seemed, drawing on his pipe a long time before answering. "You got business there, I reckon?"

"Yes sir," Eli answered. "I have a friend there."

"Hmm," the old fellow replied, taking Eli's bowl from him, walking over to the pot that sat on the small stove, dishing up a second helping for Eli.

When he handed him the bowl, he asked, "You kin o' hers, if ya don't mind my askin'?"

"Hers?" Eli asked, not certain who he meant.

"The woman called Red Bird, cause o' her red hair."

"Not kin, no. Her son's my best friend," Eli answered.

"Hmm," the man intoned, studying Eli closely, before saying more. "I thought ya might be kin cause o' yer red hair." He paused, shaking his head, before continuing. "They're all dead...or most all, from what I heard. A feller stopped here who'd been at their camp just after they were attacked. Killed by the Cavalry, they were, he said. The whole lot of 'em: old ones, women and even babies. I'm sorry to be the one to tell ya, son, but I doubt yer friend's alive. It'd be a miracle, if he was." He took a long draw on his pipe, staring into the fire in the fireplace, his thoughts known only to him. "But the good Lord does manage a few miracles, you know, every now and then. So he might be alive. There's always a chance, ya know."

"So, do you know where their camp is...*was?*" Eli amended his words, more determined than ever to go there. He'd been told by both his ma and pa that God was a great maker of miracles, and had grown up believing it, having seen on numerous occasions the truth of it.

"Well, let me think," the old man said. "I ain't ventured too far from here since Marketa's been gone." He scratched his head, his pipe held firmly in his lips, then removed it. "They were camped, last I heard, 'bout four day's ride from here. North—northeast of here. I heard there's trouble abrewing in them there parts, though. Best ya be on the watch for it. I heard the Cheyenne, Sioux and Arapaho are all stirred up over what's been done to 'em; treaties broken, and all the buffalo slaughtered like they've been. Can't really fault 'em none for being upset. I'd be right there with 'em if I was Injun. No excuse for it, I say. Durn shame, to be sure."

Eli stayed the night, well aware that the old man was glad for the company. He was a character, to be sure, with his scalped pate and jovial manner, and Eli hoped he would get the chance to talk with him again on his journey back to Hastings. When he saddled up the next morning, he bent from his saddle to shake the old fellow's hand and to thank him for the bounty of food he'd insisted Eli take. He'd been out of food for two days before he'd come upon the cabin, and had had no luck in catching a rabbit in one of the traps he'd set during the long nights of the journey. More than once he could have shot a deer and had all the venison he could want, but he knew a shot might bring him some unwanted guests, so he had set traps instead, to no avail.

"You take care, boy. May the good Lord ride with ya," the old man said, smiling up at Eli.

"Thank you," Eli replied. Then he asked, "What'd you say your name was, if you don't mind me asking?"

"Don't mind a'tall," the old man replied. "They call me lots of names, boy. I like 'Preacher,' best."

Eli rolled over where he laid, pulling the blanket Lydia had given him up to his chin. Smiling, he thought how fortunate he was to have met Preacher, and as he thought of him he drifted off to sleep.

CHAPTER 29

Eli had traveled far by mid-day the next day, his thoughts often going back to the Preacher's scalped head. He had never seen anything like it, and prayed a silent prayer that he wouldn't meet a similar fate. The sky was full of clouds as far as he could see, and birds flew above. It was a beautiful day, and Eli wondered how men could do such a horrible thing to one another, living in such beautiful country. Preacher had blamed the white settlers who had, as he said, "invaded" the Indian's land. But how could *any* people who claimed to have belief in God do such an unconscionable thing?

Thinking this, he wondered if Johnny knew that Indians scalped their enemies. He also wondered if Johnny condoned this, since he'd been friends with the Indians since he was young. Probably not, he thought, shifting in his saddle, his stomach growling. Johnny, after all, was half white, too. He'd been brought up to believe in God. Just because he was also half Indian, it didn't mean that Johnny had such bloodthirsty beliefs. It was upsetting to Eli to realize that he questioned his friend. Johnny's been my friend for years, he thought. Once a friend, always a friend, was an old saying, and Eli was disgusted with himself for even thinking that Johnny might have changed. He thought then how difficult it must be to belong to both cultures, now that they were fighting each other. It couldn't be easy for Johnny, Eli thought. If he's even alive, that is. He hoped he was, but knew now that the chance of it was terribly slim. He wondered, too, if the fellow who told Preacher about the killings had been Jubal Cade. Sounded like it, him showing up not long after he'd seen the camp attacked, and all.

Eli took in a deep breath. As he did, he noticed how still it had become. No birds flew overhead now, and his horse seemed to be listening to something. Eli pulled up on the reins, raising up in the stirrups to look about, wishing he was not out in the open, like he was. All seemed still—too still—as he settled back on the saddle. Taking his gun from the holster, he kept silent. And then he heard it. An unmistakable moaning sound that sent shivers through him.

It had come from off to his left, and he quickly dismounted and ran—half crouched—in the direction the sound had come from. As he neared the crest of a hill, he lay flat, hidden within the prairie grasses, his heart pounding in his chest like a hammer. He crawled forward, aware of more sounds of moaning. Slowly, quietly, he crawled on. His horse knickered softly then, and he held his breath, hoping it wouldn't cause him any danger by having done so.

As he reached the crest of the hill, he saw to his surprise, a conestoga wagon just beyond. It's horses or oxen were gone, and there appeared to be no signs of life. Lifting up to survey the area, he saw that three buzzards circled overhead. It could mean only one thing, he knew, and he made his way quickly down the hill, hurrying toward the wagon. As far as the eye could see, prairie grasses waved in the slight wind, and clouds continued to blanket the sky. He wondered if there had been an accident, and he rushed past the wagon, thinking maybe he could help whoever it was that had been injured. The sight that met his eye took his breath away, and he knew it would forever be etched firmly in his mind...

A man laid beside the wagon, blood covering his chest where four arrows had been shot into him. Eli knew he was dead without a closer glance and turned to where moaning could be heard. Stepping up onto the wagon to look inside, he gasped, his stomach reeling, and fell back. He gripped the side of the frame, trying to will his stomach to settle. Noticing that his hands were shaking, he forced himself to kneel and crawl into the wagon. A pretty woman about his own age lay inside, her dress cut from her body. She had been with child, Eli saw, and the infant had been cut from her. Eli fought to steady himself, so great was his shock at seeing this. Covering the dead baby, he pulled the dress back across the woman as best he could, unaware that tears ran down his cheeks while doing so. The woman moaned and opened her eyes, staring blankly up at him. She was dying, and he wondered how she could still be alive, with what had been done to her.

"I'm here," he said, his voice shaking as badly as his hands as he looked down at her. He took her hand in his and began saying the Lord's Prayer, not knowing what else to do. She gave no sign that she heard him, or that she even knew he was there, yet he kept repeating it until he knew she was gone.

His legs barely able to support him, he climbed down from the wagon then, falling to his knees, vomiting until he had nothing left inside him. When he rose to his feet, his body was quaking, but he walked to the side of the wagon near the man's body, where he'd seen a shovel fastened.

He took up the shovel, then looked around for a burial spot. It was then that common sense came to him, and setting the shovel aside, he turned and walked back over the hill to get his horse. Obviously the Indians had wanted horses, and it wouldn't do him much good to have *his* stolen, too. He walked to his horse, still feeling shaky, then led it back to the wagon. Flies buzzed around the man, and the buzzards now landed near the body. He ran at them, waving his arms, wishing with all his heart that he had not left the farm. Wishing he had never come upon this scene, knowing he would not forget it as long as he lived. There was another side to the story now. Man's inhumanity to man wasn't one-sided; he'd certainly seen proof of that.

He shook his head, scuffing at the ground with the toe of his boot, knowing it would not be easy to dig, but dig, he did. With sorrow and anger tearing at his soul, he dug until dark, dug until his arms and back ached, sweat wetting his shirt and running into his eyes. Let them come, he thought, let those Indians return. I'll kill every one of them, and be glad I did! He wanted to shout out the pain and anger he was feeling, wanted to scream at the injustice of it. No one should die like this, he thought. Kill them, shoot them, yes! But to cut a baby out of a woman, his stomach rolled as he thought this, and he knew he was going to be sick again. She'd been real pretty, young, her whole life ahead of her. Probably excited about journeying west like so many others, to start a life on their own piece of land. I wonder who they were, Eli thought, knowing he would search their belongings so he could let their families back East know that they had come to their journey's end. Oh, I won't tell them *how* they had died...that went without saying. Just that they rested *together* in a beautiful spot, with prairie grasses covering them like a soft golden blanket, he thought.

When at last he finished burying the man and woman side-by-side, and the baby with the woman, he knelt in the dark and said a short prayer. His words were stilted, and he knew they sounded more like a bunch of words strung together, than a prayer. It'd be a long time until I can pray again, he thought, angry now at God for letting such a thing happen. Life wasn't all milk and honey, he was finding out, and he hated the reality of it. His upbringing on the farm had not prepared him for such things, and he knew he would *never see* life as he once had, would never see it as he had as a *boy*. Life was cruel, that was a fact. Life was not always church on Sundays and a loving family and comfortable home. No, life was something else, indeed, he thought.

Something he didn't want to think about. One thing *was* certain, *his* life would *never* be the same.

He slept that night beneath the wagon, a restless sleep filled with dreams that tore at him, waking him, making him cry out in fear. In the morning he looked through the wagon, his heart aching at all the evidence of the plans and dreams these folks had had. They were the O'Brien's; Mary and Ian, from Massachusetts, and had been heading for California. Eli wondered why they were out here all by themselves and not traveling with a wagon train. But it doesn't matter now, he thought, jumping down from the wagon. Glancing out across the prairie, noticing the blue sky that stretched from one side of it to the other, he mounted his horse and continued on his way. It made more sense to turn back, he felt, but he had come this far, and knew he had to be only a short distance from Standing Elk's camp...or what was left of it. He owed it to Johnny—to their friendship—to continue, he thought, and he rode on, no longer in such a hurry to find his friend. A thought had come to him as he buried the O'Brien couple and their baby. A thought that tore at his guts, sickening him. With every breath he took he had asked himself the same question: what if it had been Standing Elk's surviving warriors who had so ruthlessly killed them?

CHAPTER 30

All day Eli rode, watching both in front of him and behind. He'd had the feeling he was not alone, and could not shake it, and by mid-afternoon he was certain of it. Even his horse was skittish, and he had to talk to it to quiet it, time and time again. It wasn't normally a nervous mount, and its actions heightened his own uneasiness. Well, if they want a skirmish, Eli thought, let them come. I'll get a few of them before they get me. He reached to his holster, more than once, as the day pressed on. I'm getting as jumpy as my horse, he thought, trying his best to keep control of his feelings, the terrible suffering of the O'Brien family always on his mind.

The sun was close to setting as he dismounted to check his horse's hoof. He'd noticed that it seemed to be favoring one leg, and he knew that was all he'd need—making escape impossible—if it was lame if an attack occurred. He had no more than gotten both feet on the ground, when the most god-awful bunch of screams filled the air. The horse shied, racing away, as Eli pulled his gun from his holster and threw himself to the ground. Before he could raise his hand to shoot, Indians circled him, their horses so close to him that he could feel the heat from their bodies. He knew it would no longer be of any use to shoot. If anything, he reasoned, it would only bring down more wrath upon him.

He was even more surprised by the fact that they weren't shooting him, though most held bows. It was apparent that something was bothering them.

They gestured—talking loudly—and it was then that Eli realized the leader of the group was pointing at his hair and motioning to another brave. This Indian rode closer, his face and body painted garishly, his dark eyes piercing. He stared down at Eli. Clad in breechcloth and moccasins, his legs hanging down on either side of his horse, he looked as menacing as all the others. Glancing from one to the other, Eli didn't know what to expect. I'm going to die, he thought, yet he couldn't help wondering why they were prolonging his death. They're probably trying to frighten me, he thought, and doing a darned fine job of it, too. He remembered then that the preacher had told him that Indians admired bravery in a man—especially a white man. He'd said Indians were more apt to deal a "quicker hand" to one who was brave. Well, thought Eli, we'll just see about that, and moving slowly, he got to his feet. As he did, the Indian who had just ridden up spoke to the others, and to Eli's surprise they turned as one and galloped off. It was then that he got the shock of his life.

"Hello, Eli. What brings you out here?"

Eli couldn't believe his eyes, as he recognized the voice of his childhood friend. "Been looking for you, Johnny," he stammered, not sure if Johnny was glad to see him, or not.

"You could have been killed," Johnny stated, his voice still not sounding all that friendly.

"That's a fact," Eli said. He holstered his gun, aware of the change that had come over his friend. "I heard about the attack on your camp, heard about your ma. I'm sorry, Johnny."

"Johnny's dead. I'm called Black Hawk now," Johnny replied, throwing a leg over his horse and sliding from its back. Uncertainty seemed to stop him, for a moment, then he walked to Eli and clasped his hand, warmly. "It's good to see you, my friend," he said, at last, sounding more like his old self.

"I didn't know if you were alive, or not," Eli said. When I heard news of the attack, I knew I had to come. In case you were wounded, you see," Eli explained.

"I was not here...then," Johnny answered, his eyes filled with a sadness that now replaced the fierceness of the earlier moment. We will go to my tepee. Come. You do not have to fear my people. You are my friend. Standing Elk will welcome you."

Johnny swung up onto the back of his horse, and Eli got up behind him. Eli remembered how they had ridden an old horse at the farm one day when they were boys, and how it had suddenly taken off at a run and they had both slid off its back, landing in a deep puddle of mud. He wondered if Johnny remembered that day, but he didn't ask. Johnny wasn't the same as he'd been then. There was an anger inside of him now—an anger that shown in the paint upon his face—and could be heard in his voice. Was it *all* whites he hated now, Eli found himself wondering? He also wondered if there was any hope for their friendship. As they approached the village, a rider came toward them, leading Eli's horse. Eli slid from behind Johnny and walked to his horse, thanking the man. The man gestured toward Eli's hair, smiled, then rode back the way he had come, as Johnny dismounted.

"They seem to like my hair," Eli commented, wondering if they wished to see it hanging from a staff in front of their tepees.

"It is the same color as Red Bird's," Johnny stated, dryly.

"Your mother's," Eli said.

"Yes," Johnny answered, walking away from him.

Hurrying to catch up with him, Eli was aware of those who watched him enter the camp. Preacher had told him only a few of Standing Elk's people had survived, and that was more than evident. A group of young boys, five in all, watched him with wide eyes, talking hurriedly amongst themselves as he passed by. Women, the three he saw as he walked along, hurried into their tepees, frightened looks upon their faces. Most of the ten or so men he'd first encountered stood silent as he followed Johnny, their faces no longer friendly, as Johnny had once told him they always were when someone new came to the camp. Now the older ones were cautious, it seemed, and the ones he guessed to be about his age looked none too friendly. It was apparent to Eli that his presence was tolerated, but not appreciated.

Stopping at a decorated tepee, Eli entered behind Johnny, seeing that it was Standing Elk's lodge. Johnny spoke in Lakota to the chief, explaining that Eli was his friend and had come to visit him. The old chief motioned them to sit and took up his pipe. "It is good that the friend of Black Hawk comes to visit," the chief said, taking a puff on the pipe and then handing it to Eli.

Eli took the pipe—seeing Johnny nod at him—then he smoked, very glad that he didn't have a coughing fit. "Thank you," he said, looking at Standing Elk and then at the paintings on the walls of his tepee. Eli had never been inside a tepee before, and was surprised at how comfortable it was.

"These are sad times," the chief said, his voice low. "The braves wish to go to war against the Bluecoats, though we have always been at peace." He hesitated a long time, then added, "Now it is time."

Eli wasn't sure just what he meant, but did not say anything. He knew very little of Indian ways, only what he'd been told, and so he made no comment.

Soon after, he and Johnny left and walked to Johnny's tepee. Upon entering, Eli was surprised to find a lovely Indian woman there. She handed them bowls of food, though Johnny didn't introduce them. Surprised by how hungry he was, Eli finished the food quickly. He saw that Johnny's tepee did not have the paintings inside, like in the chief's lodge. He wondered why, but did not ask. He felt uneasy here, uneasy even with Johnny. It was as if they were mere acquaintances and not the best of friends. Johnny not only sounded different, but he looked so unlike himself—his eyes more like that of a caged animal, Eli thought, a wariness filling them. The woman excused herself, smiling at them, then left. Eli looked at his friend, wishing he'd say something. It was a long time before he did.

"Are you glad to be here?" Johnny asked, his eyes narrowing.

" I'm glad to find you alive and well," Eli answered, seeing no warmth in the eyes of his friend.

Johnny grew quiet again, and Eli wondered what he could say to reach him. "I ran into Jubal—the old fellow who had your pa's medallion—remember?" Johnny nodded. "He's the one who told me about the attack. He said he watched it, but couldn't do anything to stop it. He said that white-haired fellow really must have had it in for the Indians."

Johnny straightened at hearing this. "White-haired fellow?"

Eli nodded. "The Cavalry officer who led the attack, he explained.

"I'm glad to know this," Johnny said. "I plan to kill him when I find him. His horse's shoe made a mark in the snow...next to my maw's...next to Red Bird's body. I will not forget it."

"You...weren't raised to kill, Johnny," Eli stated, his voice a mere whisper. "It isn't right."

"Tell me what is right, then. Is it right my mother was killed with one blow from this bluecoat's saber?" he jumped up, his voice growing much louder. "You are too *white* to understand, I guess."

Eli stood, saying, *"You* are white, too. Have you forgotten?" In one swift movement Johnny grabbed him, drew his knife from the sheath at his waist and held it tightly against Eli's throat. They stood that way, Johnny's eyes blazing into Eli's for what seemed like ages. Then Johnny moved away, sheathing his knife, all the while keeping his back to Eli.

"You're alive," Eli said, when his heart resumed its normal rhythm. "I've found out what I came for. In the morning I'll leave." Johnny nodded, still facing away from him, and Eli felt great sadness at the loss of his friend.

CHAPTER 31

The next morning the sky was a brilliant blue, not a cloud in sight when the two young men awoke. Eli laid on his side of the tepee, comfortable within the large buffalo robes. He'd been awake far into the night, trying to figure out what he could say to Johnny that might reach him. They'd been friends far too long to let their friendship end like this. But try as he might, he didn't know what to say or do to make things good between them anymore. The fact that Johnny had had the nerve to threaten him with his knife, showed Eli how little chance there was to fix things. No, he thought, I've done what I planned to do by coming here and seeing that he's all right. It's time I head for home. I'll be needed at the farm soon, to help with the planting. He scratched his side, stretching beneath the buffalo robe, his thoughts turning to the couple he had found, killed by the Indians. Once again he wondered if Johnny—or 'Black Hawk,' as he now called himself—really had been one of those who had killed them. He knew the Johnny *he* had known would have fought to the death to save them. But this man called Black Hawk...well, he wasn't sure just what *he* was capable of.

He raised a hand to his throat, rubbing the area where Johnny's knife had lain across his skin. Outside the tepee he heard the sound of others stirring, dogs barking, and someone laughing softly. He wondered about the woman who lay on the other side of Johnny's tepee, sharing his buffalo robe. He wasn't sure if she was Johnny's wife, or just some woman he'd taken up with. She was a pretty gal, had long black hair and gentle eyes that reminded him of a doe, and sure was pleasing to look at. She had two children; a baby boy and a little girl. They slept together on the other side of their mother. They didn't look like Johnny, having stronger Indian features. Eli wanted to ask about them, wanted to know about his friend's life here with the Indians. But it was too late now. That time was past. He was leaving today. Going back home to the farm, wishing he had never ventured from it.

"You awake?" Johnny asked, his voice practically a whisper as he turned his head to look at Eli.

"Yes. It's time for me to go," Eli replied, sitting up and pulling on his boots and shirt.

"Yes," Johnny stated, making no attempt to stop him.

"I'm sorry for your loss," Eli said, keeping his voice low so as not to wake the children. The little girl stirred, a long strand of black hair falling across her small face as she rolled over onto her side.

"Yes," Johnny said in acknowledgment, making no further reply.

"I wish your father could see you now, *Black Hawk*" Eli said, looking at Johnny, wishing he'd get up, get mad, anything but this total indifference.

"He would be proud," Johnny stated, tossing back the heavy buffalo hide and getting to his feet.

Eli looked at him, not saying anything. It was a look that needed no words, his meaning clear. Then he stuck out his hand and waited to see if Johnny would shake it. After a short hesitation, he did, and Eli was glad. "Goodbye, my friend. I will miss you."

Johnny said nothing, a look of indecision crossing his face, as Eli stepped from the tepee and made his way to his horse. He saddled the horse, looking around the peaceful village, then mounted. When he passed Chief Standing Elk's tepee, the old chief walked outside of it and Eli nodded at him, then turned and started the long trip home. His heart was filled with great sadness at the loss of the best friend he had ever had, and he thought it might have hurt *less*, if Johnny *had died*.

CHAPTER 32

Later that day, when the sun was straight up in the sky, Johnny found himself racing like the wind. He had been listening all morning to a lecture from Chief Standing Elk. Of course the chief looked on their talk as more a "lesson," having a wisdom seldom seen in others. It was known that he often shared his wisdom with those who needed it, and Johnny was no exception. After the lesson was given, Johnny had quickly mounted his horse and raced away, hurrying to catch up with Eli. The chief had hinted, in that wise way of his, that Black Hawk's friend was heading into trouble. At first Johnny had appeared disinterested, but as Standing Elk told him of the signs he had seen, Johnny knew he had no recourse but to get to Eli as soon as possible. He was a skilled tracker and knew he could find him. With his horse's hooves pounding the ground in time with the beating of his heart, he raced along, slowing only long enough to make certain of Eli's trail.

As he raced along, Standing Elk's words of the value of true friendship, came back to him. He had spoken of the grief now felt by those who had lost someone in the attack and that they carried their grief with dignity, knowing those dear ones were now in the next world. His way of looking at death gave Johnny a measure of peace, and he knew that he had only been thinking of himself, not others, as he wallowed in self pity. He thought then how Eli, who had never traveled far from his family farm, had ridden many many days to see if he was all right. And he was ashamed at how he had treated him, ashamed that he had not told him how grateful he was, or how he had so often wished Eli was there so he could talk to him; sharing his feelings and sorrow, like they had always shared, ever since they were young. With silent prayer upon his lips, he prayed it was not too late to reach his friend, not too late to tell him the things of his heart.

Far away to the southeast, Eli was racing for his life, arrows hitting the ground all around him. He had come over a hill, straight into a frenzied band of painted Indians who had apparently killed a family of settlers, their plunder now worn by some of the Indians. Surprised, Eli had whirled his horse around and began searching for shelter. He knew there might be little time before one of their arrows found its mark. Bending low over his horse's neck, he urged the animal on, the sound of his pursuers sending chills through him. They wore their hair in a different style than Standing Elk's tribe had, and Eli wondered if they were the same Indians who had killed the family he had buried. If they were, he was certain he would meet the same torturous fate...and soon. Seeing a great rock formation to his left, he spurred his horse on, racing for it, hoping to reach it and find safety among the rocks, if an arrow didn't find him first!

As he reached the base of the rock, he jumped from his horse, seeing how lathered it was from running. He scrambled up among the rocks, never looking back, knowing by the sounds that the Indians weren't that far behind. Then, halfway to the top, an arrow found its mark. Pain shot through Eli's body as the arrow struck him, going through his thigh and lodging there.

He cried out in pain, but forced himself to keep climbing, praying that he could make it to the top. Praying that another arrow would not hit him, all he could think was, I don't want to die here, Lord. Please don't let me die here. His mother's face came to him as he clambered up among the rocks, and then Lydia's face. They would suffer so, if he did not return. He knew that, and it grieved him.

Wedging himself behind a boulder, in a crevice that was barely big enough, he turned and began firing, seeing that his pursuers were already climbing up after him. He steadied his gun-arm, aiming, and shot. One of the Indians screamed and fell. One down, too many to go, he thought, as he aimed again.

Another Indian fell, blood spurting from a hole in his forehead. Eli moved to get a better view, bumping the end of the arrow that was lodged in his thigh, and a bolt of pain tore through him. He yelped and shot again, missing. Then he saw that one of the Indians was leaving, and as he watched, he suddenly realized that he was wrong. He wasn't leaving, he was intent on circling the rocks and coming up behind.

Eli's heart froze in his chest, hopelessness filling him. He fired again, hoping to stop the man, but to his dismay he missed again. Knowing he would have to reload he steadied his gunhand on the rock in front of him and fired again, seeing the Indian directly below him grab his chest and fall with a scream to the ground below.

With shaking hands he reached for more bullets, trying to keep his hands steady enough to load his gun. As he began, he looked up in time to see one of the Indians drop in his tracks, an arrow protruding from his back. Eli couldn't believe his eyes and took in a deep breath, wondering if he was seeing things. He knew he had lost a lot of blood; his pants were soaked all the way to his knee. Then he saw another Indian turn anxiously aside, and an arrow struck him in the chest. He plummeted from his horse, a cry sounding as he fell.

Eli finished loading, feeling faint with relief, and put a shot into the Indian who was now taking aim at someone hidden in the prairie grasses below. His bullet found its mark, and another of his pursuers crumpled to the ground. As one, the remaining Indians on horseback turned and fled. Eli sighed, resting his head upon the large boulder that was in front of him. It was then that he saw Johnny below, as he began to climb up the steep rocks toward him. Eli shook his head, smiling at his friend, and raised his hand to wave. To his shock Johnny braced himself quickly, grabbing an arrow from his quiver, placing it in readiness to shoot. Eli was too shocked to move as the arrow flew at him, whistling past his head by mere inches! Eli opened his mouth to curse, just as the body of the Indian who had circled in behind him fell with a thud, slamming into the rocks beside him. He gasped, knowing then how close he had come to dying, and that his friend had saved his life.

Danger past, the two friends had plenty to talk about, as Johnny broke the shaft of the arrow that protruded from Eli's leg, and pulled the arrow from his thigh. He stopped the bleeding, using methods he had learned from his mother, then wrapped his friend's leg. Eli had lost a lot of blood, but felt it was worth it, to have his friend back. It wasn't safe to stay where they were, knowing the Indians might return to finish the job they had started, so the two friends left the safety of the rocks. Johnny told Eli that he would see him safely to the cabin of the man called Preacher, and then he would return to Standing Elk's village. No matter what Eli said, trying to convince him to head back to Hastings, Johnny refused, saying he had no family there anymore. Eli felt sad, knowing that Johnny had not given up on his promise to avenge the death of his mother. It was obvious that no matter what he said to convince him otherwise, Johnny intended to keep that promise. And so they rode, side-by-side, two friends who had found each other again, across the miles. Yet both knew, when they arrived at Preacher's cabin, that though they would *always* be friends—they would journey together no longer.

CHAPTER 33

It was a warm and windy day in late June, and Lydia could not stop the restlessness within her. She'd been awake since long before dawn, scrubbing and sewing and filling water pails...anything to keep her mind off her son. Eli had been gone far too long, and with each day's passing she feared that he would not return. Michael heard her stirring and knew without asking what was bothering her. He stretched and yawned, then got up, knowing there was nothing he could do or say to comfort her. Just yesterday he had tried, and it had ended in him heading for the barn and Lydia slamming the door, telling him to stay in the old barn for all she cared. He knew it was worries for the boy that tormented her, knew that she'd only get more upset if many more days passed with no sign of him. More than once he wondered if he should go look for Eli, but he knew that wouldn't do. He had no idea where he was, or if he was even alive, though he didn't mention this to Lydia. That's *all* he had to say, and he knew he'd be sleeping in the barn till hell froze over. Lydia had a temper like no other gal he'd ever known. There'd be no living with her, if he even hinted at the thoughts he'd been having lately. No, he'd just keep those thoughts to himself, and pray that Eli would come home real soon. Still, he blamed himself for not searching longer, the day Eli left. How many times had he questioned himself, asking again and again, why he had given up so soon. Maybe if I'd gone a mile or so farther, he thought, maybe I would have caught up with him, talked to him, reasoned with him. But it was too late now. Now all he could do was wait and pray, though he wasn't much of a praying man. He shook his head, worry showing clearly upon his face.

"G'morning, hon," he said, walking over to Lydia to give her a kiss. "You're up early."

"Yes," she answered, reaching up to give him a quick kiss in return. She turned away then, telling him breakfast would be ready soon. He nodded, and went outside to tend to his morning ablutions, looking across the field in hopes that...but no, only a herd of deer grazed on the far side of the field near the woods. He shook his head and went to the stream. He was happy here now, living in the cabin he'd bought so long ago from the Gentrys. True, he'd let it go nearly to ruin when he was into "other things." I should have known better, he thought, but it was an adventure, riding with the gang. I might not have found Lydie if I hadn't gone to Chaska. Thinking of her, any guilt he'd felt because of his involvement with them, lessened. He knelt, scooping up the icy cold water with both hands and splashed his face, shivering slightly. Well, those days were long gone and would not happen again. He'd heard that the gang was all gone now, except that old fellow who used to tag along...Jubal...Jubal Cade. The old varmint, Michael thought. He'd trade his mother—if he had one—for a jug of whiskey. Filthy, too, you could smell him for a mile. Glad I don't have any nasty habits. He scratched himself, as he thought this, laughing, then stood again and headed for the house. It would have been awful nice to get my share of the take from the stage, though, he thought, as he entered the cabin, seeing that Lydia had breakfast on the table. He had always dreamed, since the first day he'd gone to work for the Gentrys, of someday not only owning their place, but of turning it into the largest cattle ranch in the whole area. But that took money he didn't have.

"Nice day out," he said between bites of food. "Do you need anything from town? I thought I might take the buckboard in and get some things; fence for the pasture and such."

"No," Lydia replied. "I want to stay close to home. I have some washing to do."

"It won't make him get home any quicker, Lydie, waiting and watching for him," Michael said, knowing the real reason she didn't want to leave the place.

"You go, if you want. I've got washing to hang out. Should have had it all out already. I can't just go running off to town every time you go, Michael."

"All right, hon. I know you can't. But, you can't just..."

"I have work to do," she said, cutting him off. He shrugged, wishing she'd listen to him, but it was plain she wouldn't.

"I want to replace all the old fence posts by the outhouse. Some of them are rotted clear off. A little wind, or somebody leaning on one of them, and that whole stretch of fence will go down. I don't want the horses getting out," he said, wishing she'd talk to him about what was bothering her. Maybe, if we talk, he thought, it'd help her somehow—or help me. In my own way, I'm doing my best to keep busy, too.

"When'll you be back?" she asked, running a hand through her hair. She had on a calico dress, a big white apron covering the front of it, and he thought she was as pretty as when she was a girl. Oh, how he had loved her then, sneaking out behind the barn, and over near the old mill, not to mention, in a buggy out behind the house where she lived with that namby-pamby preacher fellow, David Cole. She was quite the gal then, fiery! More gal than that churchy young reverend could handle, that was for sure. He smiled, glad that *he* was the man she was married to now. There was nothing nambsy-pambsy about *him,* and she knew it. He reached out, taking hold of the back of her dress, pulling her over to sit on his lap. "Hadn't you better get going?" she asked, wrapping her arms around his neck.

"Have you got any better ideas?" he asked, teasingly.

She giggled softly, bussing him on the cheek, then stood and pulled away from him. "Save those ideas for tonight, husband," she said, walking over to the stove, her hips wiggling suggestively.

Michael smiled, winking at her, then stood, walked over to the door and left. He whistled a tune, a feeling of satisfaction filling him.

Lydia heard the buckboard leave and quit what she was doing. She walked over to the table and sat down, laying her head on her arms. She hated the way she felt; so anxious and afraid. She'd seen a lot in her life; seen the good and bad in men, and had been treated as rough by some as could be. She knew it took all kinds to make a world, but what she'd heard about the redskins struck a terrible fear into her. She'd heard—far too many times—how they killed, raped and plundered, attacking for no earthly reason as far as most whites could tell. So there'd been a few buffalo killed, she thought. Did they think they *owned* them? White folks had a right to them as much as they did, didn't they? And now, her boy was out there looking for his friend. How long could it take? Shouldn't he have been back long before this? Unless the murdering savages had killed him, that is. She rubbed her arms, thinking this, sure that she'd go mad, if they had. If they ever found out, that is. Neither she nor Michael had any idea where he was or which way he had gone, and there was a whole country out there, just beyond the woods. She brushed a strand of unruly hair back out of her eyes and got to her feet. I don't know how much more waiting I can do, she thought. It'd be easier to just shoot myself. I could stand the pain of that. It's the pain of *not knowing* that I can't stand. She lifted the heavy basket of wet clothes and headed out to hang them.

As she hung the last garment, she heard a buggy approaching and turned, seeing it was Lilly driving it. She was alone, the look on her face nearly identical to the one Lydia wore.

"Hello," Lilly said, stepping down from the buggy and walking over to Lydia. "I thought maybe you could use some company."

"How are you? Let's go inside. There's a fresh pot of coffee on the stove—unless you'd prefer a cup of tea?"

"Coffee will be fine," Lilly said. "It can't make me any jumpier than I already am."

"Me, too," Lydia replied, giving her sister a quick hug. "Nice day for a buggy ride."

"I had to go to town, anyway. Thought I'd just come on out and see how you are. I saw Michael in town. He said he thought you'd like some company."

"Yes," Lydia replied, realizing both of them were skirting around the real reason for her visit. She could see the worry on Lilly's face—the same as her own—and knew that was the real reason her sister had come.

"We might as well say what we're thinking, Lilly," Lydia said at last. "He should have come home by now, shouldn't he?"

Lilly nodded, "I thought he'd be back in time to help his pa, to help *Jonas*," she emphasized, "with the planting. He's always the one who does the big field..." she let her words drift off, settling herself in one of the chairs at the table. She looked around, noticing how nice the cabin looked. She was pleased to see that Lydia had made a real home of the place, adding some feminine touches; curtains at the windows, and a vase of flowers over on the small table near the fireplace and on the kitchen table. Smiling, she took the cup of coffee Lydia handed her. Lydia sat down in the chair to her left, having been very aware of her older sister's appraising look around the room.

"I made the curtains," she said, after a moment. "I cut them out of an old dress that I found in the other room. Do you like them?"

"Yes. I remember that dress. It used to be Sarah's. She wasn't one to worry about curtains, was more an outdoor person," Lilly said. "You've made the place look real nice, Lydia. I'm proud of you."

"Thanks," Lydia said, pleased by her sister's words of praise. They drank their coffee in silence then, neither one wanting to discuss their worry for their son.

"I planted a garden on the other side of the cabin, where it'll get more sun," Lydia said, at last, breaking the silence. "Do you want to see it? I've never planted one before, but I remembered the one you always put in at the farm, and how nice it was to pick a fresh tomato or a handful of peas on my way out to the barn."

"I'd love to see it," Lilly said, surprised that Lydia had even remembered the garden at the farm. She had always seemed too wild, and far too interested in anything *but* the farm. They rose and walked outside, Lydia leading the way. As they came around the house, she had just begun to tell Lydia something, but as Lydia had done so many times the past weeks, she automatically glanced toward the forest on the far side of the field. Gasping, she stopped so abruptly that Lilly walked right into her.

"What is it, Lydia?" Lilly asked, and then she saw where Lydia was looking. In the distance, a rider had just left the woods and was riding toward them. It was too far to make out the man, but the horse was one she couldn't help recognizing. Her heart began racing within her, so fast that she had to steady herself against a tree, as she raised one hand to cover her mouth.

Lydia lifted her skirts above her ankles and began to run. She didn't care that it was unladylike to do so. She only cared that God had answered her prayers and brought her boy home. Running as fast as she could, she didn't stop until she was too winded to go on, and then she bent to catch her breath. When she straightened, she could see the rider clearly now. He wasn't the boy who had gone, so long ago, to find his friend. It was clear that *that* boy was gone. But in his place rode a bearded man, trail worn and weary, but home safe, at last.

CHAPTER 34

Lilly watched, from where she stood near the cabin, as Eli swung off his horse as he reached Lydia's side. She saw him take her sister into his arms and hold her a few moments. To her surprise, it did not hurt her. Lydia *was* his mother, after all, and Lilly knew how worried she had been. She watched them walk toward her then, and noticed that Eli seemed to be favoring one of his legs a bit. She noticed how tired he looked, too, and that he now sported a beard and much longer hair. He's so handsome, she thought, even more handsome, in fact, with the beard. Hearing the murmur of their voices, interspersed with Lydia's laughter, now and then, her heart brimmed with joy. She was so glad that she had chosen to come visit this very day. Then she thought of Jonas; how relieved he would be to know their son was home. Smiling broadly, she walked toward the approaching couple, seeing Eli look at her with such love in his eyes that she had all she could do, not to cry.

"Eli," Lilly said, as he stepped into her embrace, his breath warm upon her cheek.

"Hello, Mother," he said, holding her close for a long time. She wondered if he, too, was trying not to let his emotions get the best of him. "Are you well?" he said at last, stepping back from her, studying her face.

"I'm fine, son," she answered, feeling tears well-up in her eyes. "Now that you're home safe and sound, I'm just fine.

"I'm glad," he said, and he motioned to Lydia, who stood off to one side, a wide smile upon her face. "Let's go inside, ladies." Then he added, *"After* I get my gear off the horse that is, and turn him into the pasture with the others."

"I'll go heat up the stew," Lydia said, reaching to touch his arm one more time before turning away.

Eli put one arm around Lilly's shoulders, and they walked over to the barn. "How's Father?" Eli asked, noticing the flush of color upon Lilly's cheeks. "I'm sorry I missed planting season."

"He's fine. The hired man gave him a hand." Eli smiled down at her, then walked to his horse. When his saddle and bridle were off and hanging over the fence, and the horse let out into the pasture with Michael's horses, he bent to pick up his bedroll and saddlebags.

"You've hurt your leg," Lilly said, seeing the blood stains upon his pants and that he moved in a manner that favored the leg, as she had at first suspected.

"It's better than it was," he said, not wanting to upset her. They walked side-by-side to the cabin and entered, smelling the aroma of the venison stew that cooked upon the stove.

"Where's my...Michael," he corrected, thinking of all four people as his parents, yet not wanting to hurt *any* by showing favor.

"He went to town," Lydia said. "He should be home any time now. He was fretting and fussing, cause he was so worried about you, and so was I, so...well, it was *best* he went." She smiled then, and so did Lilly and Eli, both understanding her meaning.

The two women sat on either side of Eli at the table as he ate the bowl of stew and then another. They nearly overwhelmed him with the looks of love they both gave him. He had been through hell, no other word for it, and sitting here, he thought, was as close to heaven as he could now be.

"Did you...ah...find Johnny?" Lydia asked, at last, and both women saw the troubled look that crossed Eli's face before he replied.

"Yes," he answered, simply, and resumed eating. "Is there any coffee?" he asked, obviously changing the subject.

It was then that they heard the sound of a buckboard coming up the road, and knew Michael had returned. Eli stood, wiping his mouth on his sleeve, saying, "Sounds like Michael's back. I'll go see if he needs help unloading the wagon," and he pushed back his chair and went outside.

Michael jumped down from the wagon seat, walking to the side of it, intent on unloading the supplies he had gotten. He was just about to reach into it as he looked up and got the surprise of his life. "Eli!" he exclaimed, rushing around the wagon at sight of Eli walking toward him. He wrapped his arms around the man who stood before him, for only a moment. It was apparent, at first glance, that the journey had changed Eli, and Michael wondered what he had been through. "Oh, son. It's good to have you home," Michael said, grinning broadly at the younger man. "We've missed you."

"Let me help you unload," Eli said, walking over to the wagon and surveying all that Michael had purchased.

"I'm going to dig up the old fence out by the outhouse. Most of the posts have rotted off, anyway. Don't want the horses getting out. But let's not worry about it right now, son. Let's go on in, I'd like to hear about your travels. Did you find your friend? How long have you been back?"

Eli smiled, hearing the excitement in his father's voice. They might as well hear it now, he thought. No time like the present.

"Yes, I found Johnny, but there's been a lot of changes in his life. I'll help you unload after we've had a chance to talk."

They walked back to the cabin and went inside, Eli limping slightly, and Michael well aware of it. He wondered what his son had been through, also aware that there had been a lot of changes in Eli's life, too.

CHAPTER 35

His parents listened as Eli told of his travels to find his friend, hearing the sadness in his voice as he spoke. They all flinched, visibly, when he mentioned being wounded; the women's faces blanching at hearing it. He assured them he was now all healed, though there was a time—while staying at Preacher's, after—that it looked like he might be in trouble, as infection had set into his wound. He'd stayed there for weeks while the man tended him, since he knew a lot about poultices and such.

As they listened to Eli, they all were certain that he was leaving a lot of things out of the telling. He hesitated often and became quiet when asked questions. It wasn't just that he was sparing them; it was apparent he avoided certain subjects for his *own* peace of mind. When one of them asked how long he had stayed at the Indian camp, for instance, he had picked up his cup and drank from it, before saying simply, "Not long." When he was asked how Johnny was taking his mother's death, Eli had gotten a faraway look in his eyes before he replied, "Not good." When Lydia asked why Johnny hadn't come back to Hastings with him, Eli had stared out the window, then taken a deep breath before saying, "He...doesn't belong here, anymore."

Seeing his son's hesitation and discomfort, Michael stepped in, saying, "Want to give me a hand with unloading, now?" And a flicker of relief crossed Eli's face, before he nodded and stood, smiling a quick smile in the women's direction.

They unloaded all the supplies, working together as they always had, like a well-matched team. There was no need for words as they worked, and Eli felt relieved. Michael had always seemed to know just what it was he felt, and just what he needed. Given time, he would tell him more. But, for now, it was enough to just be working at his side, like he was used to doing. There was a comfort in doing this. He was grateful that Michael didn't poke and prod, asking questions that he wasn't ready to discuss. It was enough to be back, to be safe, and to be home. He knew the wound in his leg was small, compared to the wound in his heart. And until *that* wound healed, they would all have to be content with the answers he *could* give.

"I'll go home with Ma...with Lilly...tonight. Then tomorrow I'll come back and help you with the fence, if that's okay," Eli said, looking over at Michael, as they walked back to the cabin.

"Maybe you should rest up a day or two, then come out."

"No. I'd rather be busy," Eli replied, not looking at Michael. Michael stopped, placing one hand on the boy's shoulder, saying, " If you ever need to talk, son, I'll be glad to listen."

Eli nodded, then the two men went back inside.

CHAPTER 36

Jonas was walking toward the house when he saw the buggy turn into their lane, a horse tied on behind it. A man was driving, he could see as it drew near, and he wondered for just a moment who it was that had come home with Lilly. Then, suddenly, he realized that it was Eli's horse tied behind, and a grin spread across the big man's face. He wiped his hands on a cloth from his back pocket, hurrying toward the porch where he knew they'd stop, happier than he'd been in a long time.

Eli saw his pa as they turned in the lane to the farm, saw the smile appear on his face as Jonas realized he was home. Smiling at Lilly, he hurried the horse along, coming to a halt near the house and stepped down, only to find himself the recipient of a bear hug. Jonas wrapped his arms around the boy, not caring that he was a grown man and might not appreciate such a gesture. He'd been worried near sick as each day came and went, and was happy beyond words, knowing his son was home, safe and well.

Lilly felt tears well-up in her eyes as she watched them, feeling the happiness they felt. They were her men, and both so special to her.

Stepping down from the buggy, she walked over to where they stood, tears glistening in her eyes. "Well, Jonas, how do you like the surprise I brought home with me?" she asked, smiling up at her husband.

"There's none I'd like more," he said, his big hand still clasping Eli's shoulder. Like every one of Eli's parents, he could not seem to get enough of the boy...as if touching him made him really there. Jonas sniffled, gazing at Eli. "Yup, none at all, I'd like more."

They went into the house then, Lilly telling them she'd go fix a pitcher of tea. When they were alone, Jonas looked over at the boy, seeing the new beard he sported, and how much longer his hair was. He saw right away that there was a change in Eli, a change that had come from grief or sadness, he was sure. "Difficult journey?" he asked, breaking the silence.

"More than I can tell," Eli answered, his voice nearly breaking.

"Are you all right? I noticed you're limping a bit," Jonas said. "I..." Eli lowered his voice, glancing toward the kitchen before continuing, "I had to outrun some Indians. I was shot. The arrow tore through the muscle in my thigh. Ma doesn't know."

"I see," Jonas said. "Has it healed all right?"

"I got an infection in the wound. Johnny got the bleeding stopped, but by the time we got to Preacher's cabin—where I've been laid up a few weeks—it was pretty bad. Preacher's an old fellow who lives in Indian territory a distance from here."

"Maybe your ma or Doc should take a look at it," Jonas said. "No. It's fine now. Doesn't hurt anymore," Eli said. Then he continued, "I hear the hired man helped you with the planting. I'm sorry I didn't get home in time to give you a hand with it. If I hadn't gotten the infection, I would have been here sooner," Eli explained.

"Don't worry about it, son. I'm just glad you're home, safe and sound. That's all that matters," Jonas said, as Lilly walked into the room with a tray holding glasses and a pitcher of tea. Eli stood and hurried to take the heavy tray from her, setting it on the small table beside the chair Jonas was sitting in. Jonas poured them each a glass and they sat together, bathed in the love they all felt for one another.

"I told Michael I'd go out and help him put up fence in the morning, Pa. After that, I'll help you with whatever you need done."

"Shouldn't you just rest a day or so?" Jonas asked.

"I'd rather keep busy," Eli replied, and Jonas knew their son was having trouble adjusting to whatever he'd been through on his journey to find his friend, Johnny. It was apparent that he needed to work out his feelings on his own, and make peace with the things that were bothering him.

"If you need to talk, son, I'll be glad to listen," Jonas offered, looking over at him, a look of compassion on the big man's face.

"Thanks," Eli replied. Then he yawned, saying, "I think I'll head up to bed, if you don't mind. It's been a long day." He stood, walking over to give Lilly a quick kiss on the cheek, then went over and reached out to shake the hand Jonas offered. "I.. .I'm glad to be home," he said, looking at Jonas, who couldn't help seeing the sadness in his eyes. He'd seen similar looks on the faces of the young men he'd known in the war, and knew his son had seen things he had not expected. How bad they were, he didn't know. But he knew he'd be there to help him through, no matter when, or what it took.

CHAPTER 37

Eli arrived at Michael and Lydia's just at dawn. Michael was already out in the barn, so he unsaddled his horse and turned it out into the pasture with Michael's horses, then walked to the barn. He had had a lot of trouble getting to sleep, even though in his own bed, and felt stiff and sore. He yawned, greeting Michael, who looked up in surprise as he entered the barn.

"Well, you're up early this morning," Michael said, smiling at him as he pitched a fork of manure out the back door of the barn.

"Not used to sleeping in my bed, yet," Eli answered, looking at the fencing they'd unloaded the day before. "Thought we could get an early start on the fence."

"Good idea. Have you had breakfast yet?"

"Naw, I'm not hungry," Eli answered.

"Well, I am," Michael said. "Lydie can cook an egg like no one else. She should have breakfast ready anytime now, in fact. Let's go in. I might as well warn you, though, she's got a mean temper, son, when someone refuses to eat her cooking. You'd better plan on tackling one egg, anyway, and maybe one or two pieces of bacon and some of her good sourdough bread. Otherwise, you'll be in for a tongue-lashing." He laughed, saying this, and was glad to see Eli smiled slightly, too.

"Well, maybe a few bites," the younger man agreed.

"Well, good morning, Eli," Lydia said, as the two special men in her life walked through the door. "I thought I heard a horse, hoped it might be you." She walked over, placing another plate on the table, giving Eli's arm a soft squeeze as she passed by. "It'll be ready in a minute. Michael likes a hearty breakfast, even mine," she said, joking.

"I'm not very hungry," Eli said, sitting and looking down at the empty plate. "I might be able to eat one egg, though." Lydia glanced quickly at Michael, seeing him wink. They had laid awake long into the night, talking about their boy. It had been easy to see that he was no longer the same person who had ridden off to find his friend, and it worried them. They didn't know what he'd been through, but it hadn't been good, they were sure of that. The way he answered questions was a sure sign of the change in him. Before he left, he'd often been one to go into lengthy discussions when someone asked him something. Now they felt lucky to get a word or two out of him. It was not like him, and it worried both of them. It was apparent that he'd experienced a lot on his journey, and they suspected a lot of this change had been because of Johnny. Why, they didn't know, but there was no doubt it had been upsetting, to say the least.

Lydia dished up their plates, and as they were eating, she said, "I'll bet Jonas was surprised to see you."

"Yup. I thought he was going to break my ribs, he hugged me so tight," Eli said, a quick smile upon his face. "I told him I planned to come out here and help you today, and then I'd be back to help him at the farm."

"I appreciate the help, son," Michael said, cleaning his plate.

"Eli, are you sure you're up to it? I mean, I noticed your leg is giving you some trouble," Lydia said. "Can I ask how you hurt it?"

Michael gave her a look and quick shake of his head, and Eli saw it.

He swallowed the bite of food he'd just taken, taking his time, then looked over at Michael before answering. "I told Jonas. Guess you might as well know, too, now that you've asked." He pushed his plate back, sensing his parents anticipation. Lydia wasn't like Lilly. She was hardier, having been through a lot more. He was sure she'd be able to hear the truth and deal with it. "I came across some Indians not long after I left Standing Elk's village for home. They'd just raided a settler's place, judging from the plunder they had, and well...I became their next target." He hesitated, seeing the expression Lydia wore. "I got to some rocks, but got an arrow through my leg, in the process. It bled quite a bit before Johnny showed up and helped even the odds."

"Oh, Eli, you could have been killed," Lydia said, reaching out to place her hand over his. Michael watched the boy, saying nothing.

"Johnny got the bleeding stopped, and we got out of there. We knew there was a cabin not far, where an old man lived. We went there and he doctored my leg after it got infected. I would have lost the leg, or died, if it hadn't been for him."

"I wish we could thank him," Lydia said, still holding Eli's hand. "What was his name?"

To their surprise, Eli laughed out loud. "Well, that's the funny part," he said. "He wasn't old, though he sported a thick beard that made him look a lot older than he really was. I couldn't really tell, because he always wore a coonskin cap...because he'd been scalped, you see. I'd stayed a night at his place on my way to Standing Elk's, and it was the funniest thing; when I first got there, he asked my name, but didn't tell me his. He looked at me, like he was studying me. I'd catch him looking at me when I looked up. I thought he was a little strange, but I guess that was just a habit he had. He was a trapper, from what I could tell. He'd been married to an Indian gal, he said, but she was gone. I took it to mean she was dead, but he never did say, just

187

got a sad look on his face when he spoke of her. Anyway, he told me how to get to Standing Elk's camp and when I asked him his name, he said he preferred to be called 'Preacher.'" He picked up his cup and took a swallow of coffee, then resumed talking, "When I stayed at his cabin on my way home—while he tended my leg—I asked him again, and he said it really didn't matter, but that he was real glad to know me. Then before I left, he went to check his traps, and I picked up his Bible. A piece of paper fell out—a certificate of some sort—and his name was on it. And he really was a preacher. It said he was Reverend David Cole."

Lydia dropped her cup, splashing coffee across the table and all over the two men. Her face had turned as white as her apron, and Eli thought she was about to faint.

"Mother?" he questioned, jumping to his feet, noticing as he did so, that Michael remained sitting, an odd look upon his face.

Lydia looked at Michael, who looked at Eli, and no one moved or said anything. Then Lydia stood, walking over to pick up a cloth to wipe up the mess she had made. Still, no one spoke. Eli looked from one to the other, not knowing what to say or do. He wondered what had upset his mother so.

At last, Michael spoke, "We—you're mother and I—once knew a preacher named Cole."

Eli sat back down, noticing how his mother failed to meet his eyes, her cheeks red, as were Michael's. He took a deep breath, well aware of his mother's history, realizing that had to be the reason she'd reacted as she had. He reached out, taking her hand, making her look at him. "Preacher saved my life, Mother. That's all that's important. I'm sorry that I upset you."

Lydia burst into sobs and ran outside, leaving her two men to share a second cup of coffee in total silence. She had never felt so ashamed in all her life, or so grateful. David, the husband she had done such wrong to, had 'turned the other cheek' like the Good Book said to, and saved her son's life. And he had done it, all the while aware that Eli was her son. She could not believe that he, or anyone, would be so forgiving. Sitting on a log next to the creek, a distance from the cabin, she wished she could tell Eli just how good a man this man he called 'Preacher' really was. To do so, though, would only shame her in her son's eyes and she was certain that if he knew the truth he would never love her again. It would kill me, she thought, if Eli turned away from me. How could I live with him hating me?

She saw Michael and Eli come out of the cabin and head for the barn, and knew they were going to start work. From this distance I can hardly tell them apart, she thought, and then she saw Eli turn and look for her—waving when he caught sight of her. Timidly she raised her hand and waved back. I've made so many mistakes in my life, she thought. But having Eli was certainly not one of them. She rose and began walking back toward the cabin, thanking God for her son.

The two men worked all day, stopping long enough for a bite to eat that afternoon. They had struggled in the heat of the day, digging a new hole for the outhouse, moving it, and pulling up the fence posts that hadn't already rotted away. Sweat ran down their backs and chests as they worked, but little by little they could see that they were making progress. Eli had not done strenuous work in a long time and knew he'd be plenty sore the next day, but he welcomed the work. It kept his mind off the things he would rather forget; like the O'Brien family, and how much Johnny had changed. He didn't want to think of these things, and bent his back to the task at hand, hoping to blot out such thoughts. True, Johnny had come after him, apologizing for how he had acted, and had ended up saving him from the Indians. But still, Eli thought, he had threatened my life, holding a knife to my throat. Eli swore aloud at remembering. It galled him to think Johnny had done that. Johnny, who had been his best friend for so many years. The more he thought of it, the madder he got, and he dug furiously, his shovel slamming into the earth as he worked alongside his father.

Then he stopped, having heard an odd sound as his shovel sunk into the deep hole. It was a clinking sound, like the shovel had hit a piece of metal, or even glass. He paused, then poked the tip of the shovel down into the ground again. There it was again. He pulled the shovel out of the hole, knelt, and carefully stuck his hand down to see what he had struck.

"Eli. What is it?" Michael asked, stopping his work to watch what his son was doing. "Have you struck gold?" he said, joking. Then he saw the look on Eli's face as he began to pull his hand up out of the hole. Eli was staring fixedly at what he held, not believing his eyes!

"Michael!" he gasped, as his hand cleared the top of the hole, and Michael hurried over to see what it was Eli was holding. The two men stared...unable to say a word...for Eli had, indeed, struck gold! Dumping the fistful of gold coins into his father's hands, he reached back down into the hole, extracting still another handful of the shiny gold coins, and then another...Michael found his voice, at last, and yelled for Lydia.

Lydia rushed outside, a frown covering her face as she saw Eli on his knees, and Michael dancing around like he had gone mad. She began to run toward them, thinking maybe they had been stung by a bunch of hornets. And then she saw the sun glint off the gold pieces in Michael's hands...Gold! Golden coins...both hands full of them! She squealed in surprise and joy as she saw Eli also holding a handful, a wide smile upon his face. On the ground lay a leather pouch. Spilling out of it were gold nuggets! Lydia could not believe her eyes! If anyone had come up the road right then, they would perhaps have thought they had *all* been stung, or gone mad, or were drunk—and indeed they were—drunk with unbridled happiness!

Michael's visions of the cattle ranch he had always wanted were forming in his mind—an actual possibility now! And Lydia saw in her mind the new gingham material she had seen in the Yeager's Store, the last time she'd gone into town. And Eli...well, he saw the joy his discovery had brought about and he felt like jumping for joy!

"Michael, there's still more coins. There's a whole big jar of them, by the feel of it," Eli said. Then he froze, staring at his folks, as a sudden thought gripped him. "You don't suppose..." he said, standing quickly and grabbing up the shovel. He rushed to where another post had been, the bottom rotted off and top no longer stuck down into the ground. "I'm going to dig up the rest of this post," he said, his words tumbling one over the other in his rush to begin.

"Oh, Michael!" Lydia exclaimed. "How can this be? Where did it come from?"

"I don't know, honey," Michael said. "But I know who it belongs to now—*us,* hon—*us and our boy*!" He dropped to his knees, reaching into another hole, feeling a piece of glass cut into his hand. He pulled his hand out—seeing that the cut was small—then carefully reached back down, soon bringing up another handful of coins. He was just about to tell Lydia to hold out her hands, when they heard Eli gasp and the expression on his face told them he'd found another cache.

Kneeling and reaching into the hole he had pulled the old pieces of post from, Eli grinned as he pulled out an old tin can *full* of twenty dollar gold pieces! Laughing, as they saw them, Michael grabbed up his own shovel and raced to where another broken off, rotted post had been, knowing there were ten more posts to check under, at least.

When darkness came that night, they sat at the kitchen table, stacking piles of twenty dollar gold pieces, still not believing their good fortune. Not only did they have more than enough money to build that grand cattle ranch that Michael had always wanted, but now they could give their son a start in life that few people of their acquaintance had *ever* dreamed possible. Dirt and sweat on the men went unnoticed, and jubilant smiles covered their faces as they counted. While Lydia gave silent thanks, knowing they had been blessed in more ways than one that day.

CHAPTER 38

Having left his friend at Preacher's cabin so his infected wound could be treated, Johnny headed back to Standing Elk's camp. Anxious to return, he knew there was talk of not only the Sioux, but also the Arapaho and Cheyenne gathering near Greasy Grass to fight the cavalry. Intent on finding the soldier with white hair and the mark on his horse's shoe, Johnny planned to ride with them, so he could kill him. True, as Eli had said, he was not raised to believe in killing. But it was not a matter of what he believed, it was a matter of settling the score; an eye for an eye. His mother had been cut down without a chance, and he could not let such a vile act go unpunished. He was certain the man had seen that his mother was white. Could he not have seen her lovely red hair? He had to have. And yet it had not made the slightest difference. Well, it *will* make a difference, Johnny thought, when you answer to me. I will avenge her death, and you will feel my wrath before the devil takes you home. He urged his horse on, aware that he had a long ride ahead of him.

The sun's warmth felt good as he rode along, and he thought of his friend, Eli, and hoped his wound would heal. He'd heard tell of the preacher's skill at doctoring, and felt certain that he'd know what to do. Johnny had been worried, seeing the red lines that spread from the wound, soon after they'd arrived at Preacher's cabin. He had also seen how the loss of blood had weakened his friend. I hope he makes it, Johnny thought. He knew Eli's main interest in life was farming, and it would be impossible if he lost his leg. I should have stayed a little longer, he thought. At least long enough to see if he was on the mend. But things were different now. Preacher would see to Eli. I have a responsibility to keep the promise I gave Mother, the day that I buried her, he thought. There was no turning back now. It was a son's duty to protect his mother, but he hadn't been in camp that day.

He thought then of Brave Foot, how his body had lain near Sarah's, and felt certain he'd been running to her aid when he'd been killed. I will kill 'White Hair' for you, too, my friend, he thought. He rode along, his thoughts turning back to Eli. He felt ashamed of how he had treated him the day of his arrival in Standing Elk's camp. Even more so, when he remembered how he'd held his knife at Eli's throat. He shook his head sadly, at remembering.

I have changed, he thought. Grief changed me; seeing Mother, Howling Wolf and Brave Foot, and all the others. It caused me to hate. As long as I live, I will not forget the day when I returned to camp. Even Eli knew I had changed. If not at first, he knew when my knife lay against his throat. His horse perked up its ears, and Johnny turned his attention to the present. He was in enemy territory, and well aware that whites—seeing his Indian garb—*or* enemy tribes—seeing he rode as a Sioux warrior, would *both* consider him an enemy. I'd best be on guard, he thought. He rode then, listening intently and watching for any sign of enemies. He had few arrows left in his quiver, but that didn't bother him. If close enough to an enemy, he would use his knife. He was skilled in its use, and would not hesitate.

Laughing Water's lovely face came to mind then, and he knew she would be anxious for his return. It was normal for a woman to grieve the loss of a husband a long time. But they had told the chief they wished to be married, a few weeks before, and had become husband and wife. It pleased him to be her husband, able to make love to her, at last. He was certain it would also have pleased his mother. Laughing Water was the only woman he had ever loved, and just the thought of their nights together filled him with pleasure. He smiled, remembering how shy she had been their first night. Shy and lovely, he thought, remembering how velvety smooth her skin felt as he touched her, her long glossy black hair tickling his chin as she leaned over him. He had been pleased to find her body firm, yet supple, knowing she'd given birth to two children. They had made love that night until he could no longer do so, and then she laid beside him, wrapped within his arms, satisfaction upon both their faces. He smiled at the memory of how she always came so eagerly to him, and knew that it was no wonder Brave Foot had not wanted to lose her. He felt the same.

The sound of gunshots startled him, causing him to pull up sharply on his reins. Then war cries filled the air. He wondered if it was the same Indians who had shot Eli. Taking up his bow and an arrow, he slipped from his horse and began to move with great stealth toward the sounds. He would help fight them, if it were the same ones. Especially if it was a white family they fought. I, too, am white, after all, he thought, and was surprised he'd thought this. It did not make his life easy, being both. When he'd ridden back into Standing Elk's camp and discovered his mother and the others, and the carnage the soldiers had wreaked, he had thought only as an Indian. Yet now, after Standing Elk's long talk and seeing Eli again, he found himself ready to stand with the whites. He felt at a loss to decide *where* his loyalty actually belonged, realizing he felt loyalty to *both* peoples.

Bending low, he hurried toward the sounds of gunfire. On his belly he crawled to the hill's crest, seeing from his vantage point that it was the same Indians who were shooting at a white man they had pinned behind his dead horse. The man lay on the ground, shooting with one hand, the other appearing to be caught under the dead weight of his horse. Johnny scurried back down the hill, knowing it'd be safer to join the melee on horseback, than on foot. Once out of sight, he got to his feet and ran for his horse. The element of surprise would allow him to get close enough to the attacking Indians to lessen their number, after that he would have to depend on his knife. He grabbed his horse's mane, bolting up onto it, then placed an arrow in readiness to shoot. Startling the Indians with his cries, he crested the hill, his arrow finding its mark. A shot rang out, hitting another Indian, and the remaining Indians turned as one and fled. Johnny raced toward the downed man, a distance away, fixing another arrow in readiness to shoot, if by chance the Indians returned. He saw that the man's hand was pinned under his horse, as he had thought, as he raced closer.

As he approached, the man was looking away, struggling frantically to free his hand. Johnny raced up, not realizing the impression he now gave, his bow in hand. Ten feet from the man, the man turned, looking toward Johnny—thinking he, too, was attacking. His hand came free and he raised his pistol. Johnny was about to call out that he was a friend, but as the man looked up at him, Johnny got the shock of his life!

"Pa!," he shouted, pulling up sharply, the same instant the man squeezed the trigger. A loud explosion sounded, the bullet hitting Johnny in the chest. He stared at the man before him, as if seeing him in slow motion, then tumbled from his horse, enfolded in a shroud of blackness!

CHAPTER 39

Jericho Moses LeCroix paced back and forth in his small cabin, his thoughts confused. The young man—obviously Sioux—lay on his bed in the corner. He'd heard what he'd said, too late. He had already fired his pistol, thinking the kid was just another one of those Injuns who were out for his scalp; the way he rode up, his bow drawn and all. It had shocked him when he heard the kid call him "Pa." Shocked him bad, and he wished to hell he hadn't fired. But it was too late now. Maybe he'd never know why the kid had gotten that look on his face, like he'd seen a ghost, and called him that. He continued to pace, trying to make some sense of it. Sure, he'd known a few squaws, even a Sioux, if he remembered right. He bit his lip, trying to recall when and where. A pretty gal came to mind. She had been at the fort, south of here, was named after some kind of bird; a dove or owl. He'd only been with her that one night, if he remembered right. Of course one night might have been enough...he thought...but then he realized it couldn't have been her; this kid was too old to be their son.

He walked over to the bed, looking down at the young man who lay there, his face ashen from loss of blood. Jericho picked up the basin of bloody water and walked to the door, dumping it out, then filled the basin with clean water. He'd gotten the kid back to his cabin after he'd stopped his bleeding as best he could, tossing him across his horse and leading it, always on the watch for those Injuns to circle back. If they had, they'd have had *two* scalps hanging on their belts, that's a fact. But, I couldn't just leave him out there to die. Wouldn't be long and the buzzards would come, tearing into my horse and the kid, too, if I'd left him. Besides, I have to know why he called me pa. I never fathered any children—to my knowledge—in all my days of rambling across the country. Surely would have remembered it, if I had. I'm not like my old man, Jericho thought. I'm not some drunk that doesn't care if he leaves a woman to fend for herself when she's with child.

He shook his head, anger flushing his cheeks, and walked over to the small stove, seeing if there was any food left in the pan that sat on it. He'd gotten the bullet out of the kid after he got him back to the cabin, cleaning his wound and doctoring him, as best he could. It was a clean shot, by the looks of it, hadn't torn up any vital organs as far as he could tell. The kid had bled like a stuck hog, though. If he died, it'd be from loss of blood, more than anything. He pulled the tattered blanket up across the younger man's chest, laying a hand upon his forehead to see if he was feverish.

He'd never shot a man before; not one he wanted to *live,* that is. The only ones he'd shot, he'd shot on purpose, and they'd died where they stood. He walked over to the stove, once more, deciding he'd better get something cooking...some venison stew, maybe, so he could get some broth down the kid when he came to...if he came to.

But, first things first. I'd best go back and get my saddle and gear off my horse. The kid isn't going anywhere for awhile, and probably won't come to before I get back. It's getting dark out, less chance of those Injuns catching me, if they're still around. He glanced at the young man who lay on his bed, after reloading his guns, then opened the door and went out, closing it quietly behind him.

Jericho Moses LeCroix stood six foot five inches tall in his bare feet and weighed two hundred sixty pounds, all of it muscle and bone. He was a powerful man, strong as an ox, whose size and brawn alone commanded respect from lesser men. He'd never lost a fight, and never backed down from one. In fact, he had a reputation for enjoying a good brawl, often instigating it, it was said. He was a force to be reckoned with, though patient, his self-control and tolerance for the weakness in others, a defining trait. Women were attracted to him; his features easy on the eye. Clean shaven, his shoulder-length brown hair and dark eyes caught the interest of more than one little gal in saloons. And more times than he cared to remember there'd been some nasty catfights over who would go upstairs with him.

Tough as nails in his dealings with men, he was sweet-natured and kind with the women he'd taken pleasure with. More than one of them—he'd soon realized—hankered to hitch up with him and leave the life they were living. But he'd never let his heart get involved in his dealings with any. Neither had he ever looked down at them, knowing most had had no choice but to take up the sporting life, due to circumstances beyond their control. Oh, he'd met a few he might have considered seriously as more than just a night's passing fancy. But then he'd sobered up and high-tailed it for home, grateful for his freedom. A free spirit—free to travel and explore the country—that's the life he preferred. Never allowing himself to get attached to anything or anyone, he rode alone, able to leave at a moment's notice for somewhere, with no one left crying in his dust.

He'd been on his own ever since he was twelve, when his mother, Kathleen LeCroix, had been shot during a gunfight at the saloon where she worked. He'd been upstairs at the time, busy studying one of the many books she'd bought for him, when one of the other girls had knocked on the door, crying, telling him his maw was shot. He'd dropped the book, taking the stairs two at a time, too late to change anything. Picking his mother up, he held her to him, too angry to cry. The sheriff sauntered in about that time, ordering the two cowboys who'd done the shooting to come with him to the jail. They'd been playing a game of cards and were both so drunk that they could hardly stand. The fight had started—as most did—because one called the other a cheat. His mother had rushed over, trying to calm them, and had gotten killed for the effort.

A week later, Jericho rode out of town, his life having changed irrevocably. His mother's body lay buried in the cemetery east of town. His only possessions were now strapped behind a horse he'd bought, and he was alone. The possessions consisted of a tintype photo of his mother, smiling at him with that pretty smile she had, a few clothes, and six or seven of the books she'd given him.

He had only attended school long enough to learn to read and do some arithmetic, though he was slow at that. Reading, however, was something he liked, and he often read long into the night, never able to get enough of the grand adventures the books offered. He'd considered writing a book of his own, once, but that was foolish and he knew it. Who would want to read about an orphan who set out on his own at the age of twelve, enjoyed his first gal at the ripe old age of thirteen, and hadn't had the slightest idea where to go or what to do after that? The ladies who'd worked with his mother had chipped in and given him the gift of one hundred dollars the day he'd left. One hundred dollars that he was sure would last forever. But alas, 'forever' had come real soon, and after that he'd ridden the country, looking for the no account drunk who'd fathered him. It galled him that he'd left his mother, and he hoped to find him and settle the score.

At night he'd lay abed wherever he was, dreaming of the day he'd find Moses Gentry. He'd find him and beat him until he couldn't get up. He relished the idea of his fists slamming into him, again and again, for every tear his mother had cried after he'd left. She'd loved him, she told

Jericho, and had been sure he'd marry her, then woke one day to find him gone. He'd told her he was looking for the gang who'd killed his wife. Shot her down as she crossed the road in the town they'd lived in. Told his mother that his wife had been with child when she was shot, and he'd cried and drank nearly every night, telling his sad story over and over. Jericho hated him.

Hated him for ever coming into his mother's life, and hated him even more for leaving. Jericho had never understood how a man—even a drunken one—could cry over the loss of a woman and child, and yet leave another woman with child. It just made no sense. Unless, he thought, he'd just used my mother. That had to be it. Hatred festered in him for the man who sired him, the man he had never had the chance to know. His mother had told him once, when he was real young, that Gentry hadn't known she was with child when he left, but he didn't believe it. He thought she was just trying to temper his hatred for his father. She'd always tried to make him see life in a way that focused on the good, and overlooked the trials and tribulations. She'd been a good mother, doing what she did because she'd had no choice; her folks having died when she was young. Having no money or place to call her own, she'd found the only job she had any talent for...always hoping and dreaming the day would come when some cowpoke would offer her, and later, him, her bastard son, Jericho, another kind of life.

Jericho scanned the hillside, seeing that already the buzzards had begun their work on his dead horse. The horse had served him well, and he hated knowing that it had taken an arrow meant for him and had died because of it. Well, it could have been me, he thought, and he knew just how close he had come to dying. Stealing from the safety of the trees, he moved quickly, alert to any danger. It took all his strength and effort to pull the saddle from under the horse, but he did so, after a struggle. Then he took off the bridle and grabbed up his saddlebag and other gear, hurrying back to the safety of the trees. It was nearly dark now, but that was no sign those Indians weren't still nearby, just waiting for another chance to add his scalp to their collection. He hunkered down, listening, one of his guns at ready. All was still. One of the buzzards returned, landing beside his horse, ready to gorge himself on it. Jericho holstered his gun, picking up his saddlebags and settling his things on the boy's horse, glad it wasn't the least bit skittish. He was anxious to get back to the safety of his cabin, knowing without the horse, *he* would have had to carry everything.

He thought then of the young Indian that he'd shot. If he dies, Jericho thought, I'll keep his horse. It's a strong animal, about the same size as the one I lost. If he lives, I'll have to go scare me up one. Maybe go steal one from the Injuns who killed mine.

With only the light of the moon to guide him, he rode in silence, coming at last to the cabin. He stayed off to one side, studying it and his surroundings a few minutes, making sure he had no unwanted company. Then he dismounted, leading the horse over to the small corral where he'd kept his horse. Gathering up his belongings, he walked to the cabin, glad to get inside. He dumped his saddle and gear on the floor in one corner, lit the oil lamp that sat on the small table in the center of the room, then walked over to his bed to check on his patient.

The boy was still alive, though he felt warmer. Jericho knew his chance of surviving was slim, if he became fevered. "I'd better get that stew cooking," he said, knowing the boy would need sustenance to keep his strength up, if he was to live. Washing his hands in a pail of water by the stove, he glanced over at the small table, seeing the book that lay open upon it. He'd wanted to spend the evening reading.

He'd been right at the part where the hero in the story was heading for the bank, hoping to surprise the men who were robbing it. It had been hard to stop reading there, but he'd forced himself to do so, deciding to head on out and see if he could get himself a deer. He was running low on meat, and the way the sun was shining made it the perfect day to hunt.

He hadn't counted on running into that band of Injuns when he cleared that hill a distance from his cabin. He'd been thinking of Abbie, the little widow gal he'd visited a few days before at the trading post. She was a sweet gal with laughing eyes and moves that made the long trip there well worth it. Lost in his reveries, he had darn near rode right up to that pack of savages before he saw them. It had cost him his horse, and almost his life. It was then he remembered that the kid had shot one of the Indians when he came racing over the hill, startling them with yells of his own. If it hadn't been for that, I'd probably be laying out there, bald as all git out and dead as my horse. I owe the kid my life.

He shook his head, wishing he'd waited a minute longer before firing his gun. But, what was done was done. Now he'd just have to do the best he could to keep him alive. He owed him that much. And if he lives, I'll have the chance to find out why he called me pa, Jericho thought, knowing he wouldn't rest easy until he knew.

CHAPTER 40

The next day Johnny opened his eyes, surprised to find himself in a small comfortable cabin. His chest hurt like hell when he tried to move, and he remembered then that he'd been shot. He turned his head to look around, scanning the unfamiliar surroundings. Being careful not to move anymore than he had to, he slid one foot off the edge of the bed, groaning as he did so, then slid the other one off. Using his arms, he rolled up onto his side and pushed himself up to a sitting position. He was shaky, he noticed, and wondered if he could stand. Taking a shallow breath, he ran a hand over the torn strips of material that wrapped around his body, seeing the dark stains of dried blood on them. Someone's done a fine job of caring for me, he thought. I hope I don't start bleeding again.

He noticed then that a bedroll lay on the floor on the other side of the small stove. Looks like I put someone out of their bed, he thought, and felt grateful. He wondered how long he'd been laid up, seeing a book laying open upon the table. He was pleased to see that someone liked to read, and because of his own love for books, couldn't help wondering what they were reading. He took in another shallow breath, then stood, very aware that he felt better laying down. At least I'm alive, he thought. He smiled slightly, thinking he probably wouldn't hurt as bad, if he was dead. Moving very slowly, he walked over to the table to see the title of the book. He picked it up, intent on checking it out, unaware that the door to the cabin had opened.

"Don't lose my place," a man said, his voice deep, but friendly.

Johnny jumped, dropped the book, and grasped his chest, a loud groan escaping his lips. Then he turned, bracing himself with one hand on the table. He remembered the man he had seen by the fallen horse—the man who had shot him—but thought he had imagined how much he looked like his father. He made it a point to look down at the floor as he turned to face the man, then slowly looked up. The air went out of him then, and his knees started to buckle as he stared at a man the spitting image of his father. As he felt his knees buckle, the big man moved quickly to support him. "You'll mess up all my doctoring, kid, if you fall down," he said. And Johnny heard his father's voice as clearly as if his pa was standing before him. The man helped him back over to the bed, easing him down onto it.

Johnny stared, unable to say anything for the longest time. When he found his voice, he asked, "Who are you?"

"Jericho Moses LeCroix, kid," Jericho said, grinning. "Sorry about shooting you. I got the bullet out, by the way." Johnny's face paled as he heard the man's name. "You speak English," the man stated, sounding surprised. "So...what's your name?"

Johnny cleared his throat, pain tearing through his chest as he did so. "Johnny...Johnny Gentry," he said, seeing the large man's expression change to one of surprise, then a quick unmistakable flash of anger.

"Gentry?"

"I ride as Black Hawk now, friend of the Sioux."

"Forget that," LeCroix stated, pulling a chair over to the bed and straddling it. "You said your last name was Gentry?"

"Gentry," Johnny replied, seeing a flush spread over LeCroix's cheeks.

"Well, if that don't beat all," the man said, leaning back. He shook his head, staring down at Johnny, looking surprised.

"You look just like my pa," Johnny said, groaning as he moved to get a better look.

"So that's why you called me pa?"

Johnny nodded, trying his best not to groan again.

Jericho stood, walking over to the coffeepot. "What's your pa's given name?"

"Moses," Johnny replied, closing his eyes as the pain in his chest rippled through him again. Silence filled the cabin, followed by the sound of coffee being poured into a mug. Johnny shifted slightly to get more comfortable, willing sleep to come and ease his pain. The man named Jericho couldn't have looked more like Pa than if he *was* him, he thought, and he felt somehow comforted by the likeness. We all have a double, he had heard or read, and this fellow sure was proof of that. A bit taller than pa, though, he thought, and a whole lot bigger, but his pa's features were there, clear as day, no denying it, and as he thought that, he drifted off to sleep, a smile upon his face.

Jericho LeCroix wasn't smiling. Sitting at the table, he sipped his coffee, looking at the young man now asleep in his bed. He was obviously Indian, by the looks of him. About twenty, Jericho thought, maybe a bit older. He studied the boy's features, looking for—but not seeing—any similarity to him. So I look like his pa, he thought, taking another sip. *My* pa, he amended, and was suddenly so angry that he felt like grabbing the kid and wringing his neck, though he knew that was foolish, the boy not being to blame, and all. He rose and went outside, pacing to the corral and back, wanting to strike out at the injustice of the predicament he now found himself in.

 The last thing he wanted to do was look like the no account drunk that had hurt his mother so badly. As if fate hadn't handed me a rough enough deal, by never knowing the snake that fathered me, he thought, now I find out I look just like him! He paced and paced a long time, until his anger at last subsided, then walked back into his cabin. The kid was still asleep, he noticed, though groaning a lot. He walked over to stand beside the bed, looking down at the younger man. It wasn't the kid's fault that his pa was....he took in a rush of air, realizing for the first time that if Moses Gentry was *his* father *and* the kid's father, that he was staring down at his brother. A half brother and an Indian, to boot, but a brother, all the same.

He walked to the cupboard, reaching way inside and brought out a bottle of whiskey that he usually kept strictly for medicinal purposes. "I need a drink," he said, pouring himself a shot-glass full. He gulped it down and poured it full again, then thumped the empty bottle down onto the table. Stretching his long legs out in front of him, he settled back, savoring the second drink, well aware that life had a way of tipping upside down, just when you thought you had it all figured out. "A brother," he thought. "I've got me an Injun brother."

Johnny slept all night, waking just before the sun came up. Being careful not to cause himself any undue pain, he eased one foot off the bed and then the other, and slowly sat up. In the dim light he could just make out the form of the man, sleeping on a bedroll on the floor on the other side of the stove. Being careful not to make any noise, he got to his feet, badly needing to go outside. He saw the empty whiskey bottle on the table as he edged past it, opened the door, and slid out into the stillness of the morning.

There was a slight chill in the air, he noticed, but it felt good to be up and about. His horse whinnied a soft greeting at seeing him, and he made his way over to the corral. Moving carefully, he reached up to pet the horse, whispering softly to it. It nickered in response, as Johnny looked around, enjoying his surroundings. He was reminded of his family's cabin near Hastings, when he was younger. He had loved the mornings there; the sounds of birds overhead, the whisper of the wind through the trees, and the noise the creek made as it rushed along. He closed his eyes with remembering, and could almost hear his mother calling to him and his pa to come and eat, and his pa's laughter as he came from the barn, teasing her to make her laugh. Opening his eyes, he wished so much that he was back there.

"Johnny," his father's voice called, and for just a moment, his breath caught in his throat. Then he realized that the voice he heard was not his father, but the man named Jericho.

"I'm here," he replied.

"Thought you took off on me, kid. You feeling better today?"

"Some," Johnny answered, still amazed at how much the man looked like his pa. A dead ringer, for sure.

"I'm not feeling all that chipper, myself," LeCroix said, and Johnny knew he meant because he'd finished off the bottle.

"Are you a drinking man?" Jericho asked, reaching up to pat Johnny's horse.

"No. My pa didn't believe in drinking. And being part Indian, I stay away from it," Johnny answered. "Never saw much sense to it."

"Is that a fact?" Jericho said. "You say your pa doesn't believe in drinking? Are you sure about that?"

"Not doesn't, *didn't*. He died in the war. I'm sure he had a drink now and then; at barn dances with my mother, or at the Lucky Lady Saloon when he first came to town," Johnny replied. "But once he got to be sheriff he stayed away from it. Said it caused a lot more problems than it solved."

"I'll go cook us up a bite to eat. I'm always hungry in the morning, especially after drinking. It'll be ready when you come in."

Johnny nodded, then walked slowly toward the outhouse at the edge of the woods. He'd noticed that Jericho asked a lot of questions about his pa and wondered why. But, living out here all alone, maybe he was just making conversation, glad to have someone to talk to, he thought. His resemblance to Pa is uncanny, though.

Soon, they sat across from each other, eating the breakfast Jericho had cooked. Johnny was surprised how hungry he was, and ate two full helpings, thanking Jericho for the food.

They talked while they ate, mostly about books. Both men were surprised to discover how much the other liked to read, and had a long discussion about the many different books they'd read over the years. Johnny soon found himself telling Jericho how he had always thought he'd be a teacher, like his grandfather had been, or a preacher. Jericho said he'd never cared much for school, that he had only gone long enough to learn to read. He admitted that he had never been much good at arithmetic, and had stayed in school only long enough to learn the basics. Johnny had to laugh, remembering how he had added the number twenty-seven to his recitation when he counted, when young.

Jericho looked at him, a quizzical expression on his face that convinced Johnny to explain. As he did, a loud burst of laughter came from his listener, and he laughed along with him. It made him feel good to talk about it, telling how his mother had been so exasperated when he did so. "I tried to remember not to add it," he said, "but it became a habit. A habit I made certain to get over, once I'd started school. Can't tell you how many fist fights I got into, because of it." Jericho laughed aloud in response, his eyes twinkling with laughter.

When his laughter stopped, he stood, taking up his plate and walking to the stove. "Want some coffee?" he asked.

"No. I think I'll lay back down for awhile. There's some fresh blood on the cloth. I think I'd better take it easy," He stood, moving carefully, and headed toward the bed.

"It's time I changed those bandages, anyway. Go ahead, lay down. I'll get a basin of clean water. Let's take a look at the wound," Jericho said, picking up the basin and filling it with clean water. He moved with ease, as if he was used to doctoring folks, Johnny noticed.

"You've done doctoring before, by the looks of it," he stated.

There was a long hesitation, then Jericho turned, his face registering a look Johnny did not understand. Coming over to the bed, Jericho looked down at the younger man a moment before answering. "I knew a fellow, way back. He taught me all about poultices and the "fine art" of cleaning wounds, sewing up cuts, and setting broken legs and such. I learned a thing or two from him; things that came in handy later, during the war. He died in my arms at Williamsburg. You're not my first gunshot wound, you see. But I couldn't save him, though I tried. I always thought—when I was young—that someday I'd become a doctor, but that was just a dream, nothing more. If, he'd lived..." His words drifted off as he unwrapped Johnny's dressings, and Johnny couldn't help but see the look of sadness on Jericho's face.

CHAPTER 41

It rained the next three days—a hard rain filled with thunder and lightning—and the two men eased into a friendly camaraderie, often laughing together at one or the others reminiscences. Johnny told Jericho of his friendship with Eli Hart, expounding upon their rough beginning and many fights. Jericho told how he had to sit in the corner at school for a week, because he'd put a snake in the drawer of the teacher's desk. She was a real pretty gal, he said, and he'd gotten the idea from the book he'd been reading. He thought when she saw the snake and screamed, he'd jump up, grab the snake, toss it outside, and forever be her hero. It hadn't worked out as he'd planned, though, and she had never forgotten it or forgiven him for the fright he'd given her. They talked about a lot of subjects, skipping around the main one.

The day the rain finally stopped, Jericho was in a surly mood when Johnny woke. All night he had lain awake, wondering about the man who had fathered him. It was apparent to him that Johnny was his brother, but the kid seemed to think of him as only his father's double. It irked him, for some reason. A lot of things concerning Moses Gentry irked him, and he decided he'd had enough of wondering and guessing about the man. "Grub's ready," he growled, setting two bowls upon the table. Johnny got up, surprised by Jericho's tone of voice. Walking to his place at the table, he couldn't help noticing that he felt better than he had in a long time.

"What's eating you?" he asked, looking over at the scowling man, seated across from him.

"We've been sashaying around some things, kid, that's what," Jericho answered, taking another bite of food.

"Well, say what's on your mind," Johnny said, also taking a bite. "What's bothering you?"

"Your *pa,* that's what's bothering me," Jericho stated, leaning back in his chair, looking at Johnny.

"My pa?" Johnny questioned.

"I'm tired of jawing about everything under the sun, kid, but what we should be talking about."

"What do you mean?" Johnny asked. "Because you look like him, you mean?"

"You got that right," Jericho said. "Because I look like him."

"We all have a double, they say," Johnny said, no longer interested in eating.

"*Double*, my behind!" Jericho blurted out, slamming a fist down on the table, making the bowls jump from the force of it.

"You better tell me what you're getting at," Johnny stated, knowing he'd been wondering a few things himself. Even the fact that they both liked to read, for one thing. He'd never met any other man that loved books and reading like he did, until he'd met Jericho.

"Where did your pa live before he came to Hastings?"

"I'm not sure. I'd heard he just drifted from place to place," Johnny said. "He'd had a bad time of it; had been married before and his wife had been killed."

"*How* was she killed?" Jericho asked, tensing.

"Shot by a gang, my grandpa told me," Johnny replied.

"She was pregnant then, right?" Jericho questioned.

"Yes. It nearly destroyed Pa. He followed that gang for years, Grandpa Angus said, vowing to kill them."

Jericho stared at Johnny, knowing he had been right. It was the same story that his mother had told him, of the man that had gotten her with child and then left. But one thing still bothered him; Johnny was obviously Indian, no doubt about that, and Jericho's father had been white. It must be that Johnny's mother was Indian, he thought. "So your pa came to town and met your ma there?" he asked.

Johnny nodded.

"Your ma was Indian, but she lived in town?" Jericho asked.

"No. Ma wasn't Indian. My pa was, on his mother's side," Johnny said. "I ended up favoring her. Pa looked white."

Jericho studied the younger man. His mother had said his father was grieving the death of his wife and unborn child. That they had been killed when a gang robbed the bank and shot his wife down as she waited to cross the street to join him. There couldn't have been two men, he doubted, named Moses Gentry, who had both lost their wife and unborn child in this way. It was too much of a coincidence.

He got up, clearing the table, his thoughts unsettled. "My mother told me the same story about my pa," Jericho said at last.

Johnny stared at him, too surprised to speak. Immediately he thought of stories he'd overheard of his father, and of all that had happened before he'd come to Hastings. There was no mention of any other woman, or a son; *another* son. He shifted in his chair, trying to remember anything that might prove—or disprove—the possibility of it.

"I never met the man who fathered me," Jericho said. "He was a low down drunken snake, who left my mother when she got in the family way, and it broke her heart. I've looked for him for years, to settle the score."

"Pa wouldn't have left. He wasn't like that," Johnny said, his voice raising as anger flared in him. "He was a *good* man, an honest, caring man. He would *never* have left a woman if she was in the family way."

"When did he arrive in Hastings?" Jericho asked, pouring them both a cup of coffee, his voice calming, somewhat.

"Pa came to Hastings in 1847, I think. I heard later that he'd been hunting the men that killed his first wife for nine or ten years before that" Johnny replied, remembering.

"I'm thirty-five," Jericho said. "Was born in 1841. It looks like you and I are brothers, kid, just like I thought. The years your pa was drinking was when he met up with my ma, and fathered me, I guess. I always hated him for leaving us. Wanted to find him and beat him for hurting Ma like he did." He shook his head, thinking back to the days when he was young, and how much he had hated Moses Gentry. "You said he was sheriff, if I remember right?" Jericho questioned.

"Yup. The best sheriff Hastings ever had," Johnny said, proudly. "Hastings wasn't the same, once he left for the war."

Well, it looks like the hand of fate brought us together, kid," Jericho reached a hand out toward Johnny. "I carry my mother's family name, LeCroix, Johnny. But sure as all git out, you're my brother."

Johnny took Jericho's hand, a hesitant smile upon his face. The day he'd buried his mother, he'd felt about as alone as a man could be, knowing he no longer had any living relatives. Now, by the strangest of coincidences, he had come upon a man who had not only shot him at first sight, then doctored him back to health, but a man who was the spitting image of his—-of *their*— pa. Johnny found it hard to believe.

"What are you thinking?" Jericho asked, seeing the expression on the younger man's face.

"Just how strange life is," Johnny replied. "What if I hadn't gone after Eli when he rode away from Standing Elk's village? What if we hadn't gone to Preacher's cabin, and I hadn't heard those Indians that were attacking you, on my way back to Standing Elk's?" He paused, a smile spreading across his face, "I might have ridden on, never discovering our connection. I'm glad to meet you, *brother*," he said, and the two men shook hands, then sat there, drinking their coffee, awed by the facts as they now knew them.

CHAPTER 42

Time passed as Johnny recuperated from his wound. It was now the last day of June, and he was getting more than anxious to return to Standing Elk's camp, and to his wife, Laughing Water.

Long into the night, many nights, the brothers sat talking; telling each other of their lives before they met. Jericho found himself getting a completely new outlook concerning his father, Moses Gentry; the man he had hated for so long. And Johnny grew to respect Jericho, in spite of the stories he told of fights he had been in, and the rough-shod manner in which he had lived. He understood now how different their upbringing had been, and that Jericho had done the best he could to survive as a young boy. The many things they had in common also surprised them; their love of reading and passion for books, their habit of weighing situations before getting involved, and how both were quick to anger, although their anger soon abated.

Johnny told Jericho about his mother and how she had chosen to return to live with the Indians after his pa was lost in the war. He told him about searching for Moses; riding for days, weeks and long months, following every lead—even the slimmest, always hoping that he would find him. He told him, too, of Hastings; of the folks that lived there, and especially about his grandparents; John Bruce, and Angus and Rosie MacGregor. Jericho listened, wishing that he had gotten to know them and had shared the happy times Johnny spoke of. Instead, he'd drifted from town to town in a manner similar to their pa's, never knowing where to go next. Doing odd jobs, he had lived wherever he could find shelter, and never let anyone get close to him. He had traveled the length and breadth of the land with no destination in mind, finding comfort where he could, though alone, always alone.

And now things were different. Through a strange twist of fate, he'd discovered a brother. A brother half Indian, but a brother, all the same. I wouldn't have believed it possible if someone had told me this would happen, he thought, studying the kid who sat across from him at the table. Hell, I can hardly believe it now.

"So, when do you plan to leave for the village?" he asked.

"Soon," Johnny replied. "Guess you're about ready to throw me out." He smiled, saying this.

"I'm in no hurry to see you go. It looks like you're healing all right, now. I figured you'd be leaving, that's all," Jericho said.

"There was talk among the braves of..." Johnny hesitated, "of a big uprising of the different tribes; Arapaho, Cheyenne and Sioux, against the cavalry. I plan to ride with them. I want to find the soldier that killed my mother."

"And what will you do, once you find him?"

"Kill him," Johnny stated, a fierceness showing in his eyes that Jericho had not seen before. Jericho put down his mug, aware of the danger Johnny would face.

"It might be best to let it go, kid," he said, at last.

Johnny stared at him, surprised by his words. "Would *you* let it go, if it was your mother?" he asked, rising quickly from his chair.

Jericho took in a deep breath before answering, knowing the kid was riled. "I felt just like *you*, Johnny, when *my* mother died." He hadn't told Johnny about his mother, but felt he should now. "My maw was shot by a drunk, in the saloon where she worked. She got between two men when they started to fight, accusing each other of cheating at cards. One of the other gals came upstairs to our room, telling me she'd been shot. She died in my arms a few minutes later."

He picked up his cup, taking a sip of the coffee that had grown cold. I had no one, no family, nobody. A week later I was out of there, on my own. But not before I decided to kill the man who had killed my maw. I got the gun Maw kept in a drawer near her bed and raced over to the jail. I told the sheriff I wanted to have a word with the two men, and he let me go in back, never suspecting I planned anything more."

A loud braying laugh from Jericho surprised Johnny, as he sat back down at the table. "I ranted and raved, telling those two old coots how much my maw meant to me. Telling them that I was alone now, and it was all their fault, as if they didn't know it. I was real worked up, kid. I raged at them, not even sure which one of them had pulled the trigger. The madder I got, the less that mattered. I wanted revenge. I wanted to shoot *both* of them and make them hurt like I was hurting."

"Finally, I pulled out the gun, pulled back on the hammer and..." he paused for effect, "shot. The man closest to me screamed and backed away. His face an image I'll never forget; his eyes wild with fear—or anger—I never did find out which." He laughed again, then continued, "Before I could shoot again, the sheriff ran in, grabbed me—*and the gun*—*threw* me up against the wall so hard that I thought he'd cracked my skull. Come to find out, the two men I'd been so furious at, *weren't* the two who'd been at the saloon. Those two were in another cell near the back of the jail." He laughed again and Johnny joined him.

"I would have hung, the sheriff said, if I'd killed them. Luckily, my shot had gone wild, scaring the devil out of the man I'd *tried* to shoot, and he'd wet himself, yelling all kinds of threats at me. The sheriff shoved me out of there, telling me he ought to lock me up for what I'd done, but if I left peaceable-like, he'd let me go."

He stood, walking over to look out the window, thinking he'd heard something. "Anyways, kid, I did as he said and rode away—shaken, sad, and still angry, but glad that I wasn't gonna hang for shooting the wrong man. I had a sour taste in my mouth about the whole thing, but I figured, somehow, that Maw had probably been looking out for me from up above. She never did like violence, and would have been appalled at what I'd tried to do."

Johnny stood, walking over to stand beside him, thinking he'd heard something, too. He opened the door a crack, glancing out toward the corral, noticing the direction that his horse was looking, its ears up and eyes alert. "Looks like we've got company," he said, shutting the door, heading for his bow and arrows.

"Grab the rifle, kid," Jericho said, checking his guns. "Probably the same bunch of Injuns that were after me the other day, coming back to get our scalps."

"I hope they don't try running off with my horse," Johnny said.

"Or burning us out," Jericho added, knowing that was a major possibility. "I want to show you something, just in case," he said, and he moved quickly to the bed, yanking it away from where it sat. Under it, Johnny saw a door in the floor. "I made this opening, in case of just that," Jericho said. "It leads to a small tunnel, ending on the far side of the outhouse. If worse comes to worse, we might be able to outfox those red devils." He paused, then added, "No insult intended, kid."

"None taken, *brother*," Johnny said, grinning at him.

All of a sudden, there was the sound of gunfire, not far from the cabin, and hoof beats pounded the ground up to the door. They heard a man call out, as he threw himself from the back of his lathered mount and raced toward the cabin. Jericho threw open the door, just as an arrow hit the man in the back. He fell inside, crawling in far enough so the door could be shut, groaning in pain. Johnny was surprised to see that it was the preacher, and wondered if Eli was dead or alive.

"About twenty of those red devils are out there," Preacher said, getting to his feet. He leaned against the table, feeling his chest. "The arrow didn't go through," he said. "Can one of you pull it out?" Jericho moved to do so, saying it might make him bleed.

"I'm already bleeding," the preacher said, tasting blood. He braced himself against the table, glancing over at Jericho. "Yank it out! It ain't going to make any difference, one way or the other."

Jericho holstered one of his pistols, laying the other on the table, then took hold of the arrow and pulled. The preacher gasped and fell to his knees, his shirt now running red with blood. Jericho threw the arrow aside and reached to help the man up. "Can you make it to the bed?" he asked, nodding toward the bed.

"No use in laying down," the man said, a thin line of blood beginning to run from one corner of his mouth. "I'll be laying down soon enough. Help me get over by the window where I can do a little good before I meet my Maker."

Jericho shook his head, but did as the man said. Already the preacher was weakening from loss of blood, and Jericho admired him for his determination to help.

"They scalped me a few years back," the wounded man said, "and killed my woman not long after. I figured it wouldn't be long before they came back to finish the job." Johnny looked over at the man, his heart heavy, hearing all he'd been through.

"Did my friend, Eli, get away?" Johnny asked, fearing the worst.

"He left days ago. He might have met up with them devils, far as I know," the preacher stated. "I sure hope not. He was a nice kid. I knew his...folks." There was a gurgling sound then, and Johnny saw how pale the man's face had gotten. On the floor beneath his feet, a puddle of blood was forming. Johnny walked over to him, seeing his mouth move, but no sound issued forth.

"Preacher?" he said, looking at him.

"Pray for me..." David Cole whispered, slumping forward, his coonskin cap falling off, exposing his wounds from the scalping he'd gotten, years before. Johnny eased him down onto the floor.

"I will," he stated, knowing Preacher could no longer hear him.

CHAPTER 43

All hell broke loose then, as arrows hit the cabin, and shouts and screams filled the air. Jericho unbolted the door, opening it a crack so he could shoot at their attackers. Johnny hunkered down by a corner of the small window so he could fire through it. Two Indians hit the ground, no longer a threat, but more and more came, their blood-curdling yells sending shivers up the brothers' backs. Then an arrow found its mark, hitting Jericho in the shoulder and he cried out in pain. Johnny shot the Indian who wounded Jericho, cursing as he saw blood running down his brother's arm. An arrow flew through the small window, missing Johnny by an inch, and he shot again, seeing a man fall to the ground. Two more Indians ran from the shelter of the trees, heading toward the cabin, and both Johnny and Jericho fired, seeing them fall.

"We can't let them get to the roof," Jericho shouted over the noise of their attackers. "If you smell smoke, kid, get out!"

"Not without you," Johnny shouted back, seeing another Indian fall as Jericho's bullet found its mark. "Got more bullets?"

Jericho didn't answer as the door suddenly slammed into him, the force of it knocking him back. An Indian sprang at him, as another rushed inside, a raised tomahawk in his hand. Johnny fired, and the man dropped to the floor, only to have another take his place. Johnny fired again, but to his dismay, there was no loud explosion. He was out of bullets! In the far corner by the bed, Jericho was fighting for his life, his knife drawn, his arm bloody.

Johnny pulled his own knife from its sheath, meeting his opponent in the center of the room. He lashed out, just as the man swung his tomahawk at him, missing him by inches. A loud noise sounded over where Jericho and the other brave fought, and Johnny knew it was the bed slamming against the wall. He heard Jericho curse, then the Indian cry out and fall. More braves ran into the cabin, their eyes glaring, faces painted. The man with the tomahawk swung again, and only by jumping back quickly, was Johnny able to avoid being hit. He lunged forward then, his knife buried deep in his opponent's ribs.

As that Indian fell, Johnny found himself flanked on two sides by the last two braves to enter the cabin. Dodging to one side as one of them slashed at him with his knife, Johnny grabbed the arm of the other, catching him off balance, and shoved him as hard as he could into the other's weapon. He saw the horrified look on the man's face as his friend's knife sliced across his neck. Astonished at what he'd done, the Indian froze. And as he did, Jericho moved in behind him, grabbing him around the neck, quickly ending his life.

Total silence filled the cabin then. A startling silence, after all the ruckus. Then the brothers heard the sound of the Indians outside as they retreated. Johnny rushed to the door, just in time to see one of them disappear into the woods, leading his horse. He swore out loud, then glanced around, surprised by the number of Indians who lay dead. He brushed a hand across his face, realizing—for the first time—how sore his chest was where Jericho had shot him, earlier. Seeing no blood on his shirt where the wound was, he took in a deep breath and shut the door, bolting it, saying disgustedly, "Well, neither one of us has a horse now." And as he said it, he turned and saw Jericho fall to the floor beside the small stove, eyes shut, blood pooling on the floor beside him.

Hurrying to his side, Johnny knelt, speaking his name, then opened his shirt to see how badly he was hurt. On Jericho's side, in up to the hilt, was a bone-handled knife. Johnny looked around, not sure what to do. Get the knife out, he thought, then clean the wound. He hurried to a small side-table where he'd seen some cotton material laying and grabbed up a handful of it. Then he knelt by Jericho, hoping he was doing the right thing as he slowly pulled the knife from his side. Jericho groaned as blood gushed from the cut. Trying to stem the flow, Johnny pressed the cloth against the wound and held it there. Then he wound another piece of cloth around Jericho's body, trying his best not to move him any more than was necessary. After that, he cleaned and bandaged Jericho's shoulder where the arrow got him.

To his relief, Jericho opened his eyes, asking, "How bad is it?"

"I'm no doctor," Johnny answered. "If the bleeding stops, I think you'll live."

Jericho felt his side, able to tell that the makeshift bandage was already wet. He hurt like hell and couldn't help but wonder if he'd fought his final battle. The anxiety showing on the younger man's face offered no assurance. He coughed, a groan following, and moved one of his legs. "No other damage, is there?" he questioned, lifting his head to try and look down at his chest.

"Just your shoulder," Johnny replied, looking worried.

"My shoulder hurts more than my side," Jericho said, a smile flickering across his lips.

"Do you think, if I help, you can get up?" Johnny asked. "You'll be more comfortable on the bed."

"Ain't that the truth," Jericho replied, and he let Johnny help him to his feet. Blood, once more, soaked the material, and Johnny said a silent prayer as they made their way to the bed. Helping Jericho to lay down, he couldn't help wondering if he was going to die.

"Tell me what to do," Johnny said. "You've doctored some." Jericho whispered, "The only doctoring I did was for broken legs and arms, not for any inside damage."

"Well, we can't just let you die," Johnny said, walking over to the pail in the corner. Filling a pan with water, he put it on the stove to heat. When it was warm to the touch, he dipped a clean cloth into it, then hurried to the bed and began unwrapping the wound and sopping up the blood. Jericho closed his eyes, coughing once or twice, and Johnny wondered if his lung had been punctured. Gathering up more of the clean material, he did his best to stifle the flow again, the white cloth completely red by the time he'd finally succeeded.

Jericho lay still then, and Johnny hoped he wouldn't start coughing and lose anymore blood. He'd lost way too much as it was. Rummaging through the cupboard, he tried to find another bottle of whiskey, intent on having Jericho drink enough of it so he could stitch both his shoulder and the wound in his side. Both wounds had, at last, stopped bleeding. Looking as pale as death, Jericho lay still upon the bed, only moving when a siege of coughing occurred. Finding no whiskey, Johnny rifled through the top cupboard, then searched the rest of the cabin. He had never stitched up a man before, though he had seen his mother do so, and wondered if he could do it. Of course, he had no choice. The wound on Jericho's side was too big to close on its own. Johnny had to smile as the thought crossed his mind that *he'd* need the drink of whiskey, more than Jericho, before he did any stitching. But, to his dismay, he couldn't find any. Walking over to the bed, he bent low, asking, "Do you have any more whiskey, brother? I've got to stitch up your side."

Jericho moaned, slowly opening his eyes. Johnny couldn't help but notice how pale he looked. "In my saddlebag," he said, and once again closed his eyes.

Johnny raced over to where the saddlebags lay in a heap on the floor, reaching into them. In the very bottom he discovered a flask and shook it, relieved to find it full. It wasn't a very large flask, but having no idea the effect the amount in the flask might have, Johnny hoped it would be enough to at least dull the pain as he stitched.

Hurrying back to the stove, he cleaned the blade of his knife, then took some sinew and an awl from a small box he'd found in his brother's cupboard. His hands shaking a slight bit, he walked over to the bed, lifting Jericho's head, raising the flask to his lips. Jericho did not need to be coaxed. As soon as he felt the flask touch his lips, he drank thirstily, as though he was parched. He drank all of it, smiling happily as he finished. Johnny again wished that he'd had some of it, himself.

Taking a deep breath to steady himself, Johnny unwrapped the bandages and began to sew. The gash required many stitches, and he worked diligently, making small stitches that he was certain even his mother would have been proud to see. Jericho had cried out when he began, but after that he lay still, soothed by the whiskey, it seemed.

When he finished, Johnny felt happy with the job he had done and was relieved to see that Jericho showed no ill effects. Cleaning up the bloody cloths and any mess that required it, he soon put a pot of coffee on the stove to boil, and tried to decide what to fix to eat. It had been a long time since he'd eaten, and his stomach rumbled when he thought of food. It was time he got something cooking, not only for him, but for Jericho, too, when he came around.

Stretching, he rubbed his chest, glad that *his* wound had healed and that he hadn't had to be stitched. It was funny, he thought, first Jericho has to tend my wounds, then the tables are reversed and I'm tending to his. I hope I do as good a job caring for him, as he did for me. He looked over at the man who lay abed, noticing that he was snoring. He saw the resemblance again, between Jericho and his father—couldn't help noticing it. He wondered then, if his father had died immediately after he'd been wounded at Gettysburg, or if he had laid there in pain, his thoughts of their home and his family.

Johnny shivered at these thoughts, sadness filling his eyes. He hoped that if his father *had* lived after being wounded, that someone had been there for him; had knelt beside him and comforted him. He remembered the day he'd seen his pa's medallion hanging from the neck of Jubal Cade. Dear God, he thought, please don't let it have been Jubal who was there. But he remembered then that Jubal had said he couldn't tell who the man was who wore the medallion; his face being damaged too badly.

Johnny took in a ragged breath, looking over at Jericho. I wish my mother could have met you, he thought. I wish she could have had the comfort I feel, seeing your likeness to Pa. He gazed down at the floor then, wondering if she *would have* felt better seeing Jericho, knowing that his pa had fathered *another* son. A son, not like *me,* Johnny thought, who resembles our Blackfoot Indian grandmother. But a son who resembles Pa, so much, that it hurts and heals at the same time. These thoughts in mind, he walked over to the cupboard to get down a mug. "I don't know why you gave Jericho and me a chance to meet, God," he said, his words a mere whisper, "but I, for one, am sure glad you did. Thank you. Please don't let him die."

Hearing a noise outside, Johnny rushed to the window and looked out. There in the yard stood his horse, a long rope dangling from its neck. Johnny looked about, seeing no sign of their attackers. Grabbing his bow and arrows, he opened the door and went out. His horse pawed the ground, snorting, as Johnny reached its side. Talking softly, he led it to the corral, turning it out into it. Then he surveyed his surroundings, noticing the Indian dead that lay in front of the cabin. He patted the horse, then walked over and began gathering up arrows. He'd run low on arrows during the fight to save Eli, and hadn't had time to make more. He hurried from body to body, gathering up all the arrows he could find. We might be out of bullets, he thought, but we'll have more than enough arrows, if they return. Back inside, he glanced over at Jericho, then began hauling, first Preacher, and then the dead Indians outside. Nearly too tired to finish the job, he dug a hole and buried Preacher, writing Reverend David Cole—and the date—on a board cross, to mark his grave.

Bone tired, he walked back inside, his thoughts suddenly on his wife, Laughing Water. He wondered how she was, and if she thought he was dead. It had been so long since he'd seen her. She would have expected him to return *weeks* before. He saw, in his mind, her gentle brown eyes and lovely skin—so warm to the touch—and how eagerly she came to him. The thought of her stirred a hunger in him and he wished he was with her; holding her, making love to her, her soft cries of delight, music to his ears. Taking in a deep breath, he wondered, too, when the tribes would ride against the bluecoats. He hoped he could return in time to ride with them. In spite of Jericho's story, he felt an obligation to settle the score with the white-haired soldier who had killed his mother. He could not forgive and forget, like his brother had, when *his* mother was killed. It was *not* the same. My mother was killed *deliberately* by that soldier, not by accident because she got between two men who were fighting. It wasn't the same thing, at all, Johnny thought, knowing he wouldn't rest until his mother's death had been avenged!

CHAPTER 44

Due to his strength of character and fortitude, Jericho Moses LeCroix was up and about three days later. He still had an occasional coughing spell that threatened to lay him low, or at the least, to open the stitches where Johnny had so carefully sewn him together. He was a quick healer, however, and often laughed aloud as they discussed books, though he held a hand over the knife wound in his side, to ease the pain while doing so.

He told Johnny about his days in the war and how difficult it had been to see the men around him die of wounds and dysentery. It became apparent very soon that he was a man who liked peace and quiet, though he wasn't averse to a good fight, now and then. He'd had his share of those, he told Johnny, and Johnny could not help but hear the pride in his voice as he spoke of them. He'd been a hell-raiser, that was for sure. Johnny found himself admiring his brother, realizing how different his life had been. Oh yes, he and Eli had had their share of fights when he was younger. How many times had they stood together against some of the Hastings' bullies? But, for the most part, Johnny had avoided fights. More often than not, he had spent his time studying and reading anything and everything he could get his hands on.

Right from the first day his mother had taught him to read, books had become his life, and he had vowed to follow in his grandfather's footsteps, becoming a teacher. Jericho, on the other hand, had to learn the fine art of fighting, having no one to stand with him once he was on his own after his mother had died. Time and time again, he bore the brunt of some brutes viciousness and had to defend himself to survive. It made for a difficult life, but strengthened his determination to persevere. It also, in some odd way, taught him to have tolerance for lesser men. Those who couldn't fight back, who cowered in the face of adversity, learned soon enough that he would watch their backs if they were in the right.

Because of the life he had lived, he had become a decent man, a man his mother would have been so proud of. Johnny was proud to call him 'brother,' but felt bad, knowing their time together was running short. He missed his wife and her little ones, and every day the longing in his heart to be with her pulled at him. He'd been away from them far too long, not knowing if they were alright or not, and it worried him. He also knew, with the weather now warm, that it would not be long before the tribes headed for their confrontation with the bluecoats, if they had not already done so. He did not want to miss it. Knowing how the soldiers were—always attacking as a group—he was certain that it would be his only chance to find the white-haired soldier whose horse's shoe made a certain print upon the ground. *If* he could find him, at all, that is. He knew he would certainly try.

Jericho walked toward the outhouse, listening to the sounds of birds in the trees. It was a beautiful sunny day, nice and warm, and he no longer hurt when he coughed, which he often did. He wondered where Johnny was and when he'd return. Johnny had left that morning to buy a horse and some supplies from the trading post a good distance from the cabin. He hoped the kid would have no trouble, and would return safe and sound. He'd wanted to go with him, but Johnny said he didn't want a 'sick old man' dragging along, slowing him down on the trip. Jericho had slugged him, playfully, as he said this, telling him he might be older, but he was twice the man Johnny was. They sparred a few minutes, being careful not to do any damage to Jericho's stitches. Then Johnny shook his hand, looking at him a long time, and walked to his horse and rode off. Jericho had told him to go to the Whiskey River Trading Post and ask for Miz Abbie, the little widow woman who ran the place. He said to tell her he was LeCroix's brother, and she'd see to their list of supplies and the obtaining of a fine horse. Johnny had blushed—to Jericho's surprise—as he told him to stay overnight and enjoy her favors, if he wished. That he'd surely have *no* regrets, if he did so.

Abbie was just about the best comfort a man could enjoy between here and the Mississippi, he'd told him, laughing as the kid's face reddened. Johnny had thanked him for the suggestion, reminding him that he was married and had no need to go looking for *comfort*, since he'd soon be heading back to his wife. Jericho shook his head, smiling. "Looks like my brother doesn't like a *variety* of comforts," he said aloud, knowing *he'd,* had his share, and wouldn't have had *any* hesitation about staying overnight with sweet little Miz Abbie.

CHAPTER 45

Late at night, days later, as Jericho paced back and forth, not able to sleep due to worry because Johnny still had not returned, he thought he heard the sound of a horse and rider. Hurrying to the window, he peered out, relieved to see it was Johnny. Rushing outside, he took the saddlebags full of supplies that Johnny handed him and carried them into the cabin. Johnny led the two horses over to the corral and turned them into it. Then he walked, slowly, to the cabin. The minute Jericho saw his face, he knew there'd been trouble. There was a large bruise on one side of Johnny's forehead, and another on his cheek. One eye was swollen half-shut and his lip was twice its normal size. "What happened, kid?" he asked, tossing the saddlebags onto the floor and studying his brother's face.

"Nothing," Johnny replied, turning away. "Got any coffee?"

"What? You ride into a tree, or something?" Jericho asked, not happy with the kid's tone of voice. "I want to know what happened to you! Who beat you?"

"What difference does it make?" Johnny said, sitting down. Jericho felt like smacking him, but held his temper in check. By the looks of it, Johnny didn't need *him* beating up on him, too. He got down two cups from the cupboard and poured coffee into them, handing one to Johnny. Then he sat down across from him, waiting.

Johnny drank about half of his coffee, before speaking, and when he did, Jericho knew that the beating he'd taken didn't hurt half as much as what he had discovered at the trading post.

"They're all gone," he said, at last. "My wife and her children, Standing Elk and all the People." Johnny's eyes filled with sadness and his hands shook, Jericho noticed, as he drank more of his coffee. After a long spell of silence, Johnny continued, "I went to Miz Abbie's, like you said. I gave her the list and told her your horse was dead and you wanted to buy another. She said she had a good one out in the corral; a big Bay that you had mentioned liking the looks of, the last time you were there. She started gathering up the things on your list, then three men came in. They grew quiet, watching me, and I knew I'd have little chance against them if they made trouble. She knew it, too, motioning me to go into the back—in her rooms—and to wait for her there. Then she went back out to see what they needed."

He brushed his hair back from his face, staring down at the floor, quiet for the longest time. It was so still in the cabin that Jericho thought he could hear the beating of his heart. Then, when he thought the kid would say no more, Johnny continued. "I stayed in her room, waiting for her to return. It seemed to be taking her a long time, and after awhile I opened the door and went out. Miz Abbie was standing off to one side, one hand covering her cheek where one of those fellows had hit her."

She screamed for me to run, and the fellow closest to her knocked her down. I started for him, but the other two got to *me*, first. They... won," he said, rubbing his cheek where it was bruised, trying to smile at Jericho, his smile becoming a grimace. "I fought them as best I could, thinking I'd probably die before the fight was over. Then, when I could barely stand, we all heard the sound of a gun being cocked, and Abbie was standing there, holding a gun on them, telling them she'd shoot every one of them if they so much as moved their little fingers."

He paused, growing silent again, and Jericho wished so much that he'd been there. "She told them to leave and not come back," Johnny said, and one of them made a move toward her. She fired, hitting him in the arm. He screamed in pain, and that's when they knew she meant business. Gathering up their wounded partner, they lit out of there like they were on fire."

"Did they hurt her?" Jericho asked, thinking how small she was, wishing he could have been there and made those men pay for their actions.

"Bruised her cheek, is all," Johnny replied, finishing his coffee. "But that's when she told me what they were all fired up about. On the 25th of June, the Arapaho, Cheyenne, and Sioux rode against the 7th Cavalry at Greasy Grass. It seems they killed General Custer and his whole troop. It's called, by *your* people, the Battle of Little Big Horn. And now Custer is called a hero, in spite of his crimes against the Indians. *My People* are scattered to the wind; some having sought refuge in the Grandmother Land. The land *you* call Canada. Still others were forced to travel to far distant lands, or placed in reservations, no longer free to return to their homes. Those men spoke of Standing Elk, Miz Abbie told me, bragging that he and his entire village had been wiped out," Johnny said, his voice choking up, and he hurried outside, not wanting Jericho to see his anguish.

Jericho sat at the table, waiting for his brother to return. He had heard Johnny refer to 'his people,' meaning the Indians, and it angered him. He understood the grief he was feeling. Johnny had lost his wife and family, if what those men said was true. Jericho understood his pain. But he felt a greater sadness when he heard him say the entire troop had been killed. Who wouldn't be sad, hearing that?

General Custer, of course, was another case. He was known as a man who was arrogant and felt himself to be superior to others. Few men actually liked him, it was said. He walked to the stove, getting himself another coffee. He wondered what would become of the Indians now, for surely there would be severe retaliation. Washington would see to that. After all, they had to have their hero, he thought, and who better than a man who had died while fighting practically the whole Indian nation? He shook his head, wishing he could see a newspaper and read what everyone was saying.

Johnny returned, his eyes revealing his grief. He sat down across from Jericho, once more, glancing over at him with a weary look upon his face. "I have to go look for my wife and her children. I'll leave in the morning. I'm grateful for everything you've done for me..." he paused before adding, "but I guess this changes things."

Jericho cleared his throat, his anger building. "What does it change?"

"*Everything,*" Johnny said, looking down at the table.

"So that's it, kid? It doesn't matter that we found each other? Doesn't matter that we've done our best to keep each other alive?"

"Does it?" Johnny said, looking at him. "How can we go on from here, knowing what we know now?"

"Damn!" Jericho yelled, slamming his fist down on the table. "Are you too much *Indian*, kid, to be my brother, is that what you're saying? Or am I *too white* to be yours?" He got up, wanting to knock some sense into the younger man, but instead picked up the coffeepot and hurled it across the room. The coffee still in it splattered across the wall and onto the bed, as it hit the wall, bounced across the bed, and landed on the floor. "You may think you're too *red* to be my brother, kid, but you're a darned fool, if you do. Moses Gentry was father to *both* of us! He was Indian *and* white, from what you've said. Well, guess what? That makes *us* the same! You're no more Indian than I am, whether you want to admit it, or not! You want to go live with the Injuns? Well, go do it. Hunt for your wife and her kids. I hope you find them. Hunt for Standing Elk and what's left of his tribe. Do what you have to, "*Black Hawk*. Go on! Walk away from your *real 'blood brother*.' You think it'll hurt me? I was alone, kid, *long* before you came into my life. Go do what you've got to do, I don't care. But you just remember, you aren't as *red* as *they* are, no matter how much you look like them!" With that, he went outside to pace, furiously angry!

Johnny sat still, too sore to argue, too hurt to reply. I *am* red in my heart, he thought, and that was something Jericho LeCroix would *never* understand. I'm like my mother. I love the Indian people like she did. I don't need some smart-mouthed white brother telling me what to do. I got along without him, too, before we met. I can walk away and never look back, and it won't hurt one bit. He rose, looking over at the saddlebags. He's *too white* to live off the land and survive without store-bought things, he thought. He began to smile as he thought that, but his face hurt too badly, and again his smile ended in a grimace.

Deciding he'd best be moving on, he picked up his bow, filling his quiver with arrows, just as Jericho came back inside. "I'm leaving," Johnny said.

"Take care of yourself." He waited for a response, but Jericho did not reply.

Johnny turned then, and left the cabin. He led his horse out of the corral, glad that the moon made it light enough for him to see his way. Aware that he was too sore to ride any great distance, his pride would not let him go back inside. Grabbing his horse's mane, he swung up onto the animal, patting it and talking softly to it. Then he turned it toward the woods, sadness filling him.

At the edge of the woods, he turned to look back at the cabin, seeing the door was now shut and no light shown inside. He turned back, taking in a deep breath, and urged his horse on. It would be different, he thought, if we'd met while young. It would have *mattered* then. But it's too late now. We might be brothers, but we're as different as night and day.

As he thought that, he remembered how Jericho had called him by his Indian name, Black Hawk, and it made him feel a greater sadness. If Standing Elk's people were all dead as that man at the trading post had said, then I'm as alone as Black Hawk, he thought, as I am as Johnny Gentry. He shifted a bit, already beginning to feel too sore to ride, but knew it was too late to turn back. Feeling he had *no home* now—anywhere—he felt a loneliness more painful than the bruises on his body.

He thought then of the vision he'd had while he was healing from his fight with the bear, years before. *He'd* been the one who had caused the fight, not able to control his anger as he saw that Laughing Water was with child when he returned from searching for his father. Thinking she'd betrayed him, he had acted like a fool, taunting a bear until it attacked him. He hadn't cared if he lived or died, wanting only to avenge his grief. His shoulder had been ripped apart by the bear, and he'd lain in the lodge of the medicine man for three days, sometimes awake, sometimes sleeping.

He dreamt many dreams then, sometimes fighting the bear again in his dreams. Then, in one of the dreams, he'd heard the bear speak to him, asking, "Why have you challenged me, Little Brother?" And he remembered how ashamed he'd felt, then. "Is it not better," the bear had asked him, "to seek answers to the things that trouble you?"

He'd seen a mountain before him then, the peak covered with snow. And on either side of the trail through that mountain, huge rock cliffs reached up to the sky. He remembered he had felt like he was floating, up, up, amongst those cliffs. Then he'd been standing at the very top of the highest mountain, looking beyond it. A blazing sun filled the sky, and he felt the warmth from it healing him. It was then the bear came to stand beside him, though not as his enemy. Standing up on its hind legs, it pointed toward the trail. And as he watched, the trail became red—a good sign among the People—and the bear became an old man.

Johnny remembered he had spoken then, calling the man 'Grandfather,' telling him he did not understand the things he saw. As the winds blew, buffeting his body, the Grandfather told him he was to go from there during the Moon of Falling Leaves (November.) I did as you told me, Johnny thought, as he rode along. I left when you said. I did as I was told and I've suffered for it.

He saw then, the second time he'd seen the bear; the day he'd gone to the cave where he and Brave Foot had played as boys. He had implored the bear to come, and the Grandfather to tell him what to do, not wanting to hurt his friend, yet knowing how deeply he loved Brave Foot's wife. Sitting for a long time, with arms outstretched, he asked for guidance. After awhile, he saw the great bear take form before him, rising up on its hind feet. It spoke, giving him the same instructions. Telling him to go. Telling him that it was time. Telling him that there was much for him to learn. He closed his eyes, seeing clearly all that he had seen then, knowing he'd been right to leave, rather than hurt his friend. It cost me, though, he thought. It cost me my mother. Looking up at the moon, he felt anger build within him. Did you send me away to protect me? Did you think I would have left, if I'd known she was going to die? She might have lived if I had stayed. He closed his eyes, letting the rhythm of the horse carry him along, overwhelmed by both his memories and these thoughts.

After awhile, he opened his eyes, taking in a deep breath. "It is a hard lesson you've shown me, Grandfather," he said aloud. "But, I think I understand now." He pulled up, sliding from his horse. He sat upon the ground, feeling the coolness of it beneath him. No longer noticing the pain from the beating he'd taken, he was aware only of the stillness and peacefulness of his surroundings. He had been spared for a reason, he knew that now. A reason he could never have imagined. Closing his eyes, he welcomed the thoughts that now came to him...

There is a road that is easy to follow, that requires no decency, no goodness, or honor to follow it. Among the People, it is known as

the bad Black Road.

But I was shown another road...one difficult to travel. A road that has sadness, pain and hurt. Yet, it is a road of honor, truth and hope. A road the People call the good Red Road.

Johnny sat still, more at peace than he'd felt in a long time. It's all about *choice,* he thought. Man *chooses* the life he has. Every day, every decision he makes determines what his life will be. He can choose to fight, to hate, to cheat or lie. Or, to love, to care, to endure. He can choose to pray and believe, or deny and turn away, even from God.

Johnny opened his eyes, hearing his thoughts as clearly as he'd heard the Grandfather speak, so long ago. I can choose to leave and be alone, or I can stay...he did not take the time to think any farther, but got to his feet, walking over to his horse.

Mounting, he did not notice the pain from the beating he'd received. When rested and healed, he would go in search of Laughing Water and her children. He would search until he found them. But right now there was something that he had to do. Turning his horse back the way he had come, he knew he'd made a choice he would not regret; the choice to return to the cabin in the woods...and his brother. But as he turned back, he saw to his surprise, Jericho riding toward him, a smile upon his so familiar face.

THE END

THE OUTCAST SERIES
BY SUSAN ILEEN LEPPERT:

Courageous Outcast

Time of Remembering

Johnny Black Hawk

Red Road Home

From the Ashes of Avian